ADOBE MASTER CLASS

Photoshop Compositing
with John Lund

John Lund
and Pamela Pfiffner

Adobe Master Class: Photoshop Compositing with John Lund
John Lund and Pamela Pfiffner
Copyright ©2004 by John Lund and Pamela Pfiffner

This Adobe Press book is published by Peachpit Press.
For information on Adobe Press books, contact:
Peachpit Press
1249 Eighth Street
Berkeley, California 94710
510-524-2178 (tel), 510-524-2221 (fax)
http://www.peachpit.com

To report errors, please send a note to errata@peachpit.com
Peachpit Press is a division of Pearson Education.
For the latest on Adobe Press books, go to
http://www.adobe.com/adobepress

Editor: Serena Herr
Development Editor: Darcy DiNucci
Technical Editor: Victor Gavenda
Copy Editor: Sally Zahner
Production Coordinator: Hilal Sala
Interior Design: Kim Scott
Cover Design: Kim Scott
Proofreader: Darren Meiss
Index: Jack Lewis
Compositors: Chris Gillespie and Kim Scott

ISBN 0-321-20545-6
9 8 7 6 5 4 3 2 1

Printed and bound in the United States of America

For Jack and Adele, my parents,
who encouraged all of my aspirations and endeavors
(unless it had to do with motorcycles)
—John Lund

For my family, who helped me composite my life
—Pamela Pfiffner

About the Authors

John Lund has been shooting pictures professionally since 1976 and first began to use Photoshop to manipulate images on a computer in 1990. John's work has won numerous awards including the *Communication Arts Photography Annual, Print Design Annual, Western Art Director's Club*, and *PDN/PIX Digital*. He and his work have been profiled in *Professional Photographer, Macworld, PDN, Design Graphics, Shutterbug*, and many other magazines. He has written numerous articles on digital imaging, served as digital photography editor for *Digital Imaging* magazine, and taught workshops on photography and imaging for United Digital Artists, Santa Fe Workshops, Palm Beach Workshops, and others. He currently divides his time between stock photo production, travel, and his "Animal Antics Collection," a series of images featuring pets and other animals in human-like poses and situations.

Pamela Pfiffner's career in journalism encompasses print, Web, and television. She has been editor-in-chief of such magazines as MacUser and Publish. In 1997 she launched the dynamic-media Web site for cable television station ZDTV (now TechTV), and in 1999 began Creativepro.com, an independent portal for creative professionals. She writes, speaks, and consults about technology and tools for designers. Pfiffner has a Masters degree in Journalism from the University of California at Berkeley, where she also taught print and Web design and production. She now teaches at Portland State University in Oregon. Her book *Inside the Publishing Revolution: The Adobe Story* (Adobe Press/Peachpit Press) was named 2002 Book of the Year by Design, Type & Graphics magazine.

Acknowledgements

John Lund and Pamela Pfiffner thank:
Darcy DiNucci for her patient editing, keen intelligence, common sense, and stalwart spirit;

Serena Herr and Hilal Sala at Peachpit for guiding this book through swirling editorial and production eddies;

Kim Scott for her visual acumen and wonderful design;

Sally Zahner for her sharp-eyed copyedit;

Victor Gavenda for his technical expertise;

Christine Yarrow and Kelly Ryer of Adobe Press for ongoing support and sustenance; and

Nancy Ruenzel, Nancy Davis, and Marjorie Baer at Peachpit Press for giving this project the green light.

John thanks:
Phil Saltonstall for first pointing me in the direction of digital imaging;

Don Craig for letting me trade my photography for a copy of Photoshop;

Sue Charles for trading those early (and expensive!) SuperMac monitors and video cards with me;

Annabelle Breakey for putting up with me all these years in the studio;

Sam Diephuis and Annie Harrison for keeping the business running while I devoted myself to the book;

Dianna Sarto, my wife, for keeping the home fires burning and for all of her love, encouragement, and servings of humble pie;

My digital compatriots who have always been supportive, sharing, and inspirational: David Bishop, Gerald Bybee, Dan Clark, Helene DeLillo, Katrin Eismann, Diane Fenster, Andrew Hathaway, Sam Merrell, Ken Milburn, Andrew Rodney, Jeff Schewe, Glen Wexler, and so many others;

Mark Robyn and the crew at Robyn Color Lab for their early support;

Dan Steinhardt of Epson for his continued support assistance through the years;

Barry Haynes for giving me my first in-depth look at Photoshop;

Jano Avenessian for guiding me through the hardware maze;

Mike and Rich of Command Option for frequently coming to my rescue;

Rods and Cones for untangling my color mess;

Russell Brown...for being Russell Brown (and an inspiration); and

Tony Stone and his daughter Sara Stone for their early faith in my process.

Pamela thanks:
The folks at Adobe for consistently producing a great product, even though I curse it at times;

Jeff Lalier and Cindy Samco, my partners in creativepro.com, for picking up the pieces;

Scott Phillips at LaCie for saving me and my files from certain disaster;

Sandee Cohen, Rick LePage, Bert Monroy, David Morgenstern, Sharon Steuer, and David Zwang—this book's technical- and emotional-support posse—for dispensing advice and putting up with my whining;

David and Patricia Pfiffner for being proud of me even when I don't always deserve it;

Dennis, Debbie, Chris, Tom, and Colleen Pfiffner for making me laugh;

Michael, Star, Brent, Scott, and Nicole Pfiffner for listening to my stories (and letting me win at Sequence);

The Feminist Beer Collective for putting things in perspective;

Meara McLaughlin and family for keeping me fed while giving me the space to finish;

Grace Brophy, who lived to be 104, for being a true inspiration; and

Nancy Williams and Sandy Morrison, for still being there for me, nearly 40 years later.

Contents

Foreword

I didn't set out to create a Photoshop how-to book. And despite the how-to material contained here, I hope you'll see this book as something more. I want this book to inspire. I want it to encourage you to jump in and create your own composites, to give birth to your own visions.

I am grateful that there are people who get into the nitty-gritty, nuts and bolts of things, or else we wouldn't have programs like Photoshop. But for me what resonates is the passion to create an image and the wonder at realizing we have the means to do so in Photoshop. The creative process is more than the rote memorization of technical complexities.

This book doesn't set out to teach Photoshop—I expect anyone reading it to know how to use Photoshop's basic tools and techniques. It does explain, step by step, the tools and techniques I used for various effects. But what I hope this book really does is convince you that you don't have to be a Photoshop wizard to create your own photographic realities.

It certainly doesn't hurt to possess a storehouse of digital-imaging knowledge, but transforming your vision into reality doesn't have to be a daunting task. You can accomplish it simply by taking one step after another until the task in done. And by this I don't mean a plodding torturous march, but instead a giddy skip through the process. Working with Photoshop doesn't have to be a struggle. It can be a "wow—this is cool" experiment.

And experimentation is what making a Photoshop image is for me still, after 13 years of doing it. I make no claim to having the best answers or the fastest methods, but in this book I share with you what has worked for me. When I'm working, I will sometimes use one technique and sometimes another for the same kind of task. Sometimes I use a more cumbersome technique simply because I have forgotten about a better one.

Luckily for you, in putting this book together I had the benefit of hindsight. To demonstrate the techniques required for each image, I recreated images I had made over the years. Because I wasn't creating them from scratch, I didn't have to repeat all the experimentation that was required the first time—thankfully, because that experimentation can take an awfully long time! When making the image "Lightning Strike" (seen in Chapter 4), for example, I needed to mask out a tree. Originally, it took me two full days of trial and error before I settled on the best way to do it. This time around, the task took only about a half hour. That's the technique I show here.

I hope you'll use this book to learn some of the techniques I've found most useful in creating Photoshop composites. And I hope the examples will provide some help with situations you're encountering in your own work. Ultimately, though, I don't believe there are any secrets. There are only those who dive in and do it, and those who don't.

Jump in and do it!

—John Lund

Introduction:
The Art of John Lund

It's not often you meet someone who owes his career with Adobe Photoshop to an audit by the Internal Revenue Service. But then you haven't met John Lund—yet. A successful advertising photographer since the early 1980s, Lund had had his highest-earning year ever in 1989. By 1990, the bottom had fallen out of the U.S. economy, and he was, to put it bluntly, flat broke. "It was if someone turned off the faucet," Lund says.

But with characteristic optimism and aplomb, Lund seized the downtime to take stock of his career. That period of reflection brought him to image compositing, Adobe Photoshop—and yes, the IRS (more about that later).

Mixing It Up

Lund's career in photography began as a way to sell his magazine articles, even though he'd had little formal training as a photographer. A college graduate in English literature, he'd had dreams of being a writer. But his eyes were opened when on assignment for *Yachting* magazine in 1979. "It took me a week to write a 2000-word article, for which I was paid $200," he recalls. "It took me a day to take the photographs, and I was paid $1200 for a cover and two spreads. Plus, the yacht's owner hired me to shoot images for his personal use." Lund quickly did the math. "It was at that point that I decided to forgo the writing and focus on photography."

In the period that followed, Lund developed a successful career shooting editorial, advertising, and corporate work, with an emphasis on trade advertising. Clients included the likes of DHL, Transamerica, Bank of America, Chevron, VISA, Monsanto, Xerox, and many others. When the fateful 1990 recession hit, he decided that to differentiate his work from competitors, he would concentrate on in-camera collage and compositing—in other words, methods of exposing multiple images onto a single piece of film. Thus began Lund's foray into photocompositing

He put together a new portfolio of multiple-exposure dupes (duplicated slides) from images in his files and began to get work from the new portfolio. But, he says, "I soon found out it was one thing to comb my files for images that would work together, and an entirely different thing to have to shoot what a client wanted and make those images work together."

The picture that launched a career: Lund's first assignment was photographing boats for *Yachting* magazine. He took this shot from a helicopter hovering above.

Lund made this early composite the old-fashioned way, by creating multiple exposures and combining them onto a single piece of film.

Finding Photoshop

A friend and former assistant of Lund's suggested he investigate computer technology to create his photocompositions and pointed him toward a proprietary retouching system from Dicomed. "As soon as I saw the demonstration, I was hooked," Lund says, "but the equipment cost more than $50,000 and I was flat broke." Then another friend told him about a new software program called Photoshop that could do the same thing on an Apple Macintosh computer.

"I called Adobe and asked if the company would trade some photography for a copy of the program. The person I spoke with seemed surprised and said something like, 'You're a photographer and you're not hostile?'" Lund remembers. At the time, the traditional photographic and retouching communities were dismissive of Photoshop (just released by Adobe in 1988). Traditional photographers believed that images produced on a desktop computer couldn't match those produced by traditional film equipment and high-end imaging workstations. Image retouchers publicly espoused similar opinions, but privately had concerns that this new technology threatened their livelihoods. As we now know, their fears were justified. Today, nearly every published image in the world has been touched up with Photoshop running on a Macintosh or a Windows-equipped PC.

Lund got his copy of Photoshop and several lessons from Don Craig, an art director at Adobe. Now equipped with a little knowledge, Lund spent his last $3000 on a used Macintosh II with a monochrome monitor. "I just dived in," Lund says.

Taxing Times

Almost immediately, Lund discovered the dangers of being a digital photography pioneer. Scans cost $125 at prepress houses. Hard drives were small in capacity and big in price. Photoshop itself was a mere shadow of what it is today. "It was all hard in the early days," Lund remembers, "from convincing clients that quality work could actually be done on a computer to the endless hours of imaging. Applying the Radial Blur filter once took me 18 hours, and even then it looked awful." On top of that, he says, there was the nightmare of proofing, trying to achieve color fidelity, and dealing with prepress houses that were outright hostile.

Lund persevered. Having convinced a client, the Charles Schwab investment brokerage, to let him use Photoshop on a job, he set about producing a series of four brochure covers on a color monitor he purchased with the advance.

"I remember sitting down with two Schwab art directors, one on each side of me, and rotating a file. It took 30 minutes to finish—and then it was rotated a little too far. Another 30 minutes of rotating it back, and it wasn't long before the art directors got bored and left me to my all-nighters in my desperate attempt to finish the job on time," Lund says. After completing the first three images, Lund was informed that if he insisted on doing the last cover using Photoshop, they would take the project away from him. "I did the final image in Photoshop anyway, had a transparency made of it, and delivered it to Schwab," Lund says. "They loved it. When I rather gleefully told them I did it in Photoshop, one art director replied, 'For God's sake, don't tell anyone!'"

Lund continued to buy or barter for new equipment—anything to gain a competitive edge. But as the jobs and bills mounted up, so did the scrutiny of the IRS. With the IRS about to attach his bank account for back taxes, Lund gambled on his future. Summoned to meet with an IRS agent, he arrived with his Photoshop portfolio in hand. "I showed him

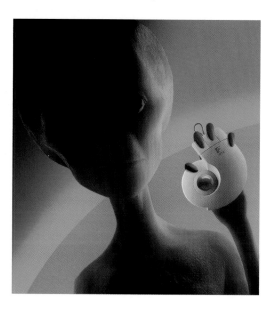

A May 1992 advertisement for a mouse and trackball from Logitech was an early Photoshop composite of Lund's. The alien was rented from a prop house.

what I was doing, and basically begged for more time because I was convinced that my work was going to take off with Photoshop and the Macintosh," Lund says. The IRS agent was so impressed with what he saw that he gave Lund another year to pay. By the end of that year, Lund's business was going so well that he was able to pay his taxes, and he never looked back.

Taking Stock

Lund realized immediately the impact Photoshop would have on his work "I could create almost any image that I could dream up, and create images that few others could. Photoshop could set me apart from my competition," he says. He also recognized its potential for opening new revenue streams. "The very first time I sat down to learn Photoshop at Adobe, stock photography came to mind. I realized that I could fix all the problems that got in the way of my images being published as stock—things like corporate logos, company labels, or badly placed telephone poles."

By 2001, Lund decided that he would focus exclusively on stock images—almost all of it digitally manipulated. "Stock photography allowed me to do the work that I wanted to do with minimal or no art direction and virtually no deadlines," Lund says. "It was the deadlines—especially in the early years, when just saving a file could take half an hour and there were no history palettes or layers to come to the rescue when you made a mistake—that made life miserable."

Lund and others of that era met with a lot of animosity from the traditional photographic community. Once when he was giving a lecture, an audience member heckled him, saying Lund wasn't really a photographer. And many stock agencies didn't want—or didn't know how—to work with digital images. Lund often had to have digital files output as transparencies from a film recorder for delivery to the stock houses.

This digitally manipulated photograph for SuperMac was one of Lund's first Photoshop-composited images.

Greetings from Photoshop-land

As a photographer and as a businessman Lund keeps seeking new ideas and opportunities. In 1998 he showed an image he had made of a smiling cat with a canary-yellow feather sticking out its mouth to Portal Publications, a company that publishes greeting cards. Lund suggested a line of greeting cards that portrayed animals in human situations or in playful poses—all digitally manipulated, of course. Portal Publications agreed, and Lund now sells as many as 225,000 "Animal Antics" greeting cards each month. The line has expanded to include figurines, posters, and more.

"'Animal Antics' represents my fourth career," Lund says. "My first career—not counting my post-collegiate stint as a self-service gas station attendant—was assignment photography. The second career was digitally manipulated assignment photography. My third career was and still is digitally manipulated stock photography. I now divide my time between producing stock images, creating animal images, and traveling, which also provides raw material for more stock imagery."

Lund's "Animal Antics" line of greeting cards shows animals in humorous situations—all digitally composited, of course.

The Easy Way

Lund's success with Photoshop compositing is all the more remarkable given that he doesn't consider himself a Photoshop power user. "I am not a highly technical person," he admits. "In 25-plus years of advertising photography, I did exactly one film test."

As a result of his resistance to the technical, Lund has devised a means of producing highly sophisticated images with relatively simple techniques. He approaches Photoshop as a photographer does, with a keen sense of light and shadow and an eye for detail. His approach may not be textbook-standard, but it works for him. And he believes it can work for anyone.

"No doubt in some ways my work would be better if I did get more precise in my methodology, but when I get caught up in the flow of work I don't want to be bothered by naming every layer and looking at histograms—so I don't," Lund says with a smidgen of defiance. "I'd say if you can do that, you'll be better off for it. But for me? I'm getting along just fine bumbling through my image making."

Lund travels around the world for inspiration and images he can use for his composites. Above and right, scenes shot in Ladakh, in northwest India.

PART I

Compositing Basics

At its most basic, photocompositing is the art of combining two or more images into a single image. A composite is not a collage, where the combining of images is obvious and artificial. Composites are meant to look real—even if the subject matter is clearly unreal.

Prior to digital tools, a composite image was created from separate pieces of film. A matte was used to hide areas not wanted in the final image. These aligned and stacked layers of film were then exposed onto a new piece of film as a single image.

Compositing in Photoshop borrows many of ideas and some of the terminology of the predigital era—but with a few differences. As with film, the core technique of compositing in Photoshop is the use of *layers* (albeit composed of pixels, not film). The layers are stacked on top of each other, and image areas are concealed or revealed using image *masks.*

Layers of Possibility

Photoshop wasn't expected to be a powerful image compositor when Ph.D. candidate Thomas Knoll began writing it in the late '80's, even though his brother and Photoshop coauthor John Knoll worked in Lucasfilm's special-effects division, Industrial Light & Magic. When Adobe licensed the product from the Knolls in 1988, the company believed it would sell at most several hundred copies a month as a photo-editing adjunct to its more-popular Illustrator application. Photoshop's immediate success soon overran that modest goal.

It was the addition of layers to Photoshop 3 in 1994 that made the application useful for compositing images. Today composite images produced in Photoshop surround us—in advertising, in art, and scandalously, in editorial material. Compositing is so popular that even budget-priced software now includes the capabilities that allow little brothers everywhere to put their sisters' heads on the bodies of cows.

Inspiration, Preparation, and Technique

Tools are well and good. But according to Lund, "Photoshop compositing is 80 percent inspiration, 80 percent preparation—and maybe another 20 percent technique." What sparks your imagination is up to you. Chapter 1 of this section deals with preparation, examining Lund's methods for capturing and collecting the images that make up his composites. Chapter 2 explores technique, offering an overview of Lund's process as he assembles images from individual parts into the final product. Then Parts II through IV take you image by image through a dozen Lund composites, showing how he conceived and then made them. Finally, Part V, the "Gallery," taps into some of that inspiration: A selection of some of Lund's other favorite images shows the magic that imagination, Photoshop, and a little compositing wizardry can conjure up.

Layers are essential to the art of compositing. They let you pile on image parts bit by bit, while letting you edit each part separately. They also let you add texture and detail, like shadows, highlights, and flying debris.

A row of abandoned phone booths in the Miami airport caught Lund's eye. "It's a great image for almost anything pertaining to communication, in particular the difficulties of communicating—and best of all, the image required no manipulation!" he says.

CHAPTER 1

Photos for Compositing

For Lund, composites—and the search for the right images—begin with an idea. Where do his ideas come from? "Everywhere—from reading and looking and listening. But I usually get my best ideas when I am in idea-hunting mode," he says—a heightened state of awareness he takes on in order to look for possible images. He has found inspiration reading an article about a motorcycle rally, seeing a line of phoneless phone booths in the Miami airport, and walking down the street near his studio.

A Search for Icons— and Sales

As a stock photographer, Lund is always on the lookout for images and subjects that are somehow iconic. "Recently I saw a water department worker in a trench digging with a shovel and throwing the dirt up on the street. I made a conscious decision to see if there was a way to turn that image, one we can all relate to, into an iconic metaphor. I ran through the scene in my mind as I went on my way, and I realized that if I reduced the scene to just the most important and simple elements I would have it. A hole, a shovel, and flying dirt! It would be an image that can represent work, an endless task, treasure hunting, or even an example of how not to get to China," he says.

As a commercial photographer, he has learned what stock images sell, and an image's sales potential is a big factor in deciding what composites he actually sits down to make. Images that clearly and dramatically express a business concept are more likely to sell as stock images, Lund believes. "I constantly make lists of what I think will work, change my mind, change my mind again, and make more lists," he says.

Lund also takes advantage of unexpected opportunities. As an example, he discovered that the company that provides him with cats, dogs, and other domestic animals for his "Animal Antics" line also had a tiger available. "I decided to create some 'tiger stock' as an excuse to justify being around the tiger," he says. Once that decision was made, he listed possible ways in which a tiger could be used to indicate business situations. "Tigers are often used to signify danger and risk. What could be more dangerous and risky than having a tiger pounce on you? So the obvious place to start is having a tiger leaping at the viewer—[stock image publisher] Corbis sells that image now. Then I thought of a tiger creeping through the grass at night and another looking intently at the viewer through a thicket of bamboo. I also made a smattering of non-composited shots, such as close-ups of the tiger snarling."

Lund steadies himself beneath a platform, as the tiger's handler tells the animal to smile.

The tiger as Lund sees it.

An already dramatic shot (above) gets even more intense with a little digital alteration (right).

Breaking It Down

Once he has an overall concept, Lund begins thinking about what component shots are needed. He sketches out the images he will need and the shots required. "When I am planning a project, I always try to figure out the simplest way to do things. I go through the process step-by-step in my mind, visualizing the image as it takes shape with each successive step. It is in this visualization that I can determine exactly what parts I will need and what characteristics those parts will have, such as the lighting, angles, depth of field, and so forth."

In "Riders" (Chapter 3) Lund envisioned a gang of motorcyclists roaring down the highway. "I see it in wide angle as the riders are almost on top of me and on each side. When I break that mental picture into parts, I see that I need a road or highway to put them into. I need the riders—some to the left, some the right, and some directly in front of me. As I won't have access to a whole gang of bikers, only one or two at the most, I will probably need to shoot other models to put their faces on a few of the riders—I can use my assistants and even myself for that. I need to shoot from a low angle, perhaps from the back of my assistant's pick-up truck. I can use a slow shutter speed to blur the riders, the road, and the background. I can use Photoshop to change the clothing colors and other details to keep it from looking like one or two riders."

Lund captures individual bikers by lying prone in the back of a pickup. Then he turns the riders into a gang in Photoshop.

In the Shadows

When shooting images that will go into a composite, Lund has a list of conditions to contend with, among them perspective, depth of field, and reflection. Planning each shot, Lund knows he'll need to keep all the parts that make up the image consistent. Light, shadow, color, and so on need to be the same for each part. "I always view the photography as the most difficult part of the procedure. That's when I have to deal with the light or weather changing, and models on the time clock going past their session," he says.

Inconsistency in light and shadow can ruin an image. "To get the right pieces, I have to make sure that the lighting is uniform. It doesn't have to be perfect, but it does have to have the same general feeling, which is primarily a matter of its direction and amount," he says. Lund is known for his consistent lighting. When possible, he mostly shoots with flat lighting that doesn't have a strong angle to it. That allows him to add contrast and shift the lighting's direction in Photoshop. This is easily accomplished by adding a highlight and a shadow to opposite sides of an object, which he does in images such "Impact" (below and Chapter 11).

Unwanted reflected light is another problem that Lund guards against, "I look for reflections that might be out of place when put in a new environment," he says. "In some cases, reflections are unavoidable, but sometimes changing the angle or even just moving something will make a big difference."

The application of highlights and shadows can transform a perfectly flat object into a spherical one—or at least give it the illusion of roundness. This wrecking ball started out as a manhole cover.

Should aberrant lighting sneak in, he doesn't worry. He knows he can eliminate it in Photoshop by adjusting the Color Balance and Hue/Saturation controls. In fact, it's possible to fix almost anything about an image in Photoshop, but Lund's attitude is "Why?" "My rule of thumb is, if it's easier to do in the camera, do it in the camera. But if it will be easier to do on the computer, do it on the computer."

Camera or Computer?

One thing that he's found easier to do in the camera than on the computer is creating an out-of-focus effect. "I have never been able to satisfactorily simulate out-of-focus effects on the computer. I have certainly done it, but it never looks *totally* real to me. So if an image is going to require an out-of-focus element I like to shoot it that way," he says. Compositing out-of-focus elements does create its own set of problems, he acknowledges. First, it can be hard to distinguish where the object's edges leave off and the background's begin when doing selections. Second, you need to give the selection and its mask a soft edge with a large feather setting to blur the edge of the mask or selection and to smooth its color transitions, and those soft edges can cause problems such as color halos around the selection. "My solution: Shoot elements both ways, in focus and out of focus. Then you can struggle through the imaging process having some options," he advises.

Another effect Lund creates with the camera when he can is perspective. Photoshop makes it so easy to move things around and distort their shapes that you may think changing perspective is a snap. But Lund finds it very complicated. "Say I am going to need a row of school desks," he says. "I could shoot one desk and then duplicate it and make the row, but the perspective would be wrong. The desks that are further to the side should show more side and less front, and that would require enormous creative illustration skills in Photoshop." If you've only got one desk (or other item) to work with, Lund suggests photographing it several times, either rotating it a bit with each shot, or better yet, setting up the camera then moving it to each spot representative of the final image before taking each exposure.

Making a Motion

Similar problems arise when trying to composite subjects in motion. If the photo isn't shot at a fast enough shutter speed, the subject will present the same selection and compositing problems as out-of-focus objects. Fringed color effects and other anomalies can show up, too. In this case, Lund says, it's easier to add motion afterwards in the computer, through Blur filters and other effects, than to go through the laborious process of somehow blending the remnants of the original background into the image.

For a composite of dogs running toward the camera, Lund photographed each dog individually at the reasonably fast shutter speed of 125th of a second, which proved to be still too slow to completely freeze the dogs' motion. "What a nightmare that was to composite," Lund groans. Unlike the "Riders" image, in which he wanted both riders and road to appear blurred with motion, he wanted the dogs to appear as if bursting from a static background. Making the edge transitions look believable was difficult. The pooches had soft, blurry edges and the background was in crisp focus. "Had I shot the dogs at, say, 1000th of a second, I could have put the image together in a day instead of a week," says Lund. "That was a case of not thinking the job through well enough." If you need to shoot a moving object for a Photoshop composite, Lund says, use the fastest shutter speed you can.

Moving subjects are challenging to composite, but Lund remembers this shot fondly: the Jack Russell terrier in the front liked to boss around the tiger he used in another shoot. (They grew up together.)

Conventional wisdom says a dominatrix and her leather gear aren't that common a sight... but anyone who's owned a cat knows otherwise.

Awareness of these issues comes with time and practice, and Lund acknowledges that he has made plenty of blunders along the way. "I can dispense this advice, because in 13 years with Photoshop, I've made all the mistakes," he says.

Spare Parts

Shooting images needed for a specific idea is just one image-gathering technique Lund uses. He also relies on "spare parts," images he shoots just in case they'll come in handy one day. He keeps an eye out for visuals that can be used as elements in a composite. "I look for textures, shapes, and interesting objects—a stormy sky, a textured wall, a bird in flight," he says. "Interesting doors, crashing waves, desert dunes, rocky cliffs, and darkening skies all come in handy." Lund shoots a lot of skies because many of his images require them, and he says you never know until you place the sky in the composite if it will work or not. "Many times I have to try five or six skies before I find one that works," Lund says. "Subtle differences in color, lighting, and gradation can really affect whether the sky will look natural or not when placed in a composite."

He used a wall he photographed in Spain 20 years earlier as the background for "Dominatrix" (Chapter 7). A lighthouse taken on assignment for a bank in the mid-1980s shows up in multiple images—often as variations on the theme of a beacon—a light in the darkness or a guiding light for navigating stormy seas. The advantage of reuse is twofold. Not shooting fresh images all the times increases his return on investment, and he saves time in compositing: Once he's gone through the effort of isolating an image like the lighthouse, he saves a copy of the file with the selection intact so he can use it again and again.

A lighthouse shot for a bank
advertisement…

…appears in one composite.

The same lighthouse from a
different point of view…

…appears in another. Reusing images is a cost- and time-efficient
way to expand your portfolio.

In parts as in final images, Lund keeps an eye out for the iconic—and flatly lit. "Not long ago I was driving past a school when I noticed a huge pile of dirt in the parking lot," he says. "I returned the next morning while the light was still low and photographed that dirt pile from every direction. That pile of dirt was so pristine and so iconic that I am sure it will come in handy someday."

These hills of dirt, shot near Lund's house, are "in the can" in case they're needed for a future composite. Lund keeps an eye out for iconic images like this, just in case they come in handy one day.

Lund always shoots more parts than he thinks he needs. "I hate to run out of parts. There is nothing worse than being in the middle of the compositing process and realizing that what you really needed was that ball shot from another angle," he says. "My advice is, always shoot more than you need, and be sure to cover all the options and variables you can."

When Lund shoots images as parts, he pays careful attention to the part's placement in the frame. He doesn't want a gracefully composed scene; rather, he wants the background to be minimal. "I try to shoot in such a way that the background won't interfere with the element in question when I go to strip it out," he says.

Parts on Disc

Lund archives his image parts onto DVD-ROM—CD-ROM is fine, too, but as Lund's images are hundreds of megabytes, he prefers the large-capacity discs. Lund advises figuring out a comprehensive naming convention and sticking to it ("something I still fail to do routinely," he adds).

For those with more money than time, you can buy images suitable for parts from stock photography agencies, such as Getty and Corbis. Buying stock images can be an economical way to fill out your parts library with everyday objects, background textures, and metaphorical icons—golden eggs, black sheep, and so on.

If you want to use such images in composites, though, make sure you buy from *royalty-free* collections, which gives you the permission to use the purchased images with more freedom than is possible with *rights-managed* images. (Rights-managed images are sold for only a specific use, and it's unlikely the agency will allow the integrity of the image to be altered. They also are often more expensive.) Even for royalty-free images, though, you'll need to read the fine print on rights and usage to make sure the use you want is allowed (see the sidebar on the next page for more on legal considerations).

Keep your image parts and finished files easily accessible by archiving them on DVD- or CD-ROM. Don't forget to label them in a consistent fashion.

Keeping It Legal

Back in the 1990s when Photoshop was gaining traction in professional imaging, questions arose about the ethics of digital photo-manipulation. Altering photographs to change the historical record is nothing new, of course; witness the removal of fallen-from-favor comrades from Stalin-era photographs or the moving of Egypt's pyramids by National Geographic magazine. But Photoshop's ease of use and the early Macintosh's low cost made digital manipulation more accessible and therefore more widespread than ever before. Photographers debate the ethics of moving a soda-pop can to create a better composition or of darkening the face of accused (now acquitted) murderer OJ Simpson on the cover of *Time* magazine.

Now that Photoshop is an accepted part of the publishing and photo-graphic process, ethical controversies are waning—some would say to such an extent that people expect images to be modified. But digital compositing raises legal as well as ethical issues. If you are not using images you created, you need to become familiar with copyright laws as they apply to images. Only the owner of the copyright can grant you permission to repurpose the work. If you did not take the photograph and you use it in your composite without permission, then you are in violation of copyright laws. It's as simple as that. The exception can be royalty-free stock photography, but even those images have restrictions.

If using pieces of objects from royalty-free stock photography collections, read the fine print in the licensing and terms of use sections carefully. All agencies impose some restrictions as to how royalty-free images can be used. For example, you can't commercially distribute royalty-free images. You can't resell them. If you make a composite image using a piece of it, you can't turn around and sell that as a stock image. Nor can you buy an image, slap it on a t-shirt, and sell it. And if a person in the image can be recognized, you can't use an image in any way that is deemed libelous, defamatory, or humiliating. Every agency has its own rules, so don't take chances: Read the rules and abide by them.

That's why it makes sense to take your own photos, as Lund does. Then you can give yourself permission to use your images in a composite.

Some digital stock companies sell libraries of image specifically made to be used as parts. Examples include the Visual Symbols Library from CMCD and the Object Series from the PhotoDisc division of Getty Images. In these collections, objects are silhouetted against a stark white background for easy selection and masking, and most even include predefined selection paths, saving you the trouble of tracing the object's contours with the Pen tool. You simply open the object image in Photoshop, go to the Paths palette menu, and choose Make Selection. The isolated object is now ready to be copied, pasted, scaled, and positioned in another document.

The Sum of Its Parts

When asked what makes an image a good candidate for compositing, Lund is typically philosophical: "An image that has impact and meaning, that's worthwhile, and that can best be achieved, either because of practicality or cost, by compositing." In other words, almost anything your imagination can dream up.

20 PART I: Compositing Basics

CHAPTER 2

Lund's Process:
From Shot to Stock

With a clear concept, a compositing plan, and the images in hand, Lund's work at the computer begins. The next sections of this book will talk about the detailed techniques used for some of Lund's images. This chapter will give an overview of Lund's general process— the considerations that go into getting an image from concept to stock house.

From Lens to File

Lund's shots are usually digital from the start: "I became a believer in digital capture early on," he says. He had one of the first digital devices that attached to the back of a film camera—the Leaf DCB—that was then tethered to a desktop computer for image uploading. It yielded a 4-megabyte (MB) grayscale file or a 12-MB color file, created by rotating a three-color wheel in front of the lens and taking one exposure each for red, green, and blue. (Many of the original images used in the composites in this book were taken with the Leaf DCB.) Despite some obvious drawbacks—three exposures meant potentially three times as many problems—Lund was hooked. "The advantages of seeing the image immediately, of not having to wait for processing or scanning, and of cost savings are too obvious to argue with," he says.

Until recently, though, he wasn't able to switch to digital photography for many images. "I wasn't happy with the newer cameras that capture

Now that he's found a digital camera that meets his requirements (the Canon EOS-1DS) Lund rarely shoots film anymore.

all three colors in one shot. The colors seemed off to me, the file sizes weren't large enough to suit me, and the lenses were not true to their focal length, especially wide-angle lenses which became less wide—and I love wide angles," Lund says.

For most of his work now, Lund ("a Nikon shooter for 27 years") uses a Canon EOS-1DS digital camera. This 11-megapixel SLR digital camera produces 31.3-MB files and lets Lund use interchangeable lenses. "For me this camera is my holy grail," he says. "The sensor chip is the same size as 35mm film, so the lenses are true to their focal length. The resulting file is of better quality than what I got scanning 35mm film, too." Lund notes that in six months something better may come along, but says, "Right now this camera is serving me very well."

Lund still uses film for special cases. "Some stock agencies flat-out won't take a digital capture—unless you can fool them, as I certainly have been forced to do from time to time," he says. He'll also use film when he wants to produce medium-format (2¼-inch) or large-format (4-by-5-inch) transparencies. When taking panoramas of skies, he has used a Fuji Panorama camera that yields 2¼-by-6½-inch transparencies, not only because it lets him take in a wider view, but also because the film grain tends to stay small even when the image is blown up.

The Right Resolution

While most of us have been taught to think of resolution as a Rubik's Cube of pixels per inch, file size, and the final print's dimensions, for Lund it's simply a matter of megabytes. "With stock images, it's impossible to know at what size a given image would be used by the client, so it's important to make sure the image has enough pixel data for good reproduction at any size," Lund explains. "In the early days most clients wanted transparencies. To output to a good 4-by-5 transparency from a film recorder, my service bureau wanted a minimum file size of 50 MB. Interestingly enough, now most of the stock agencies I deal with also require digital files that are 50 MB."

Once a film image is scanned, you can change its dimensions by changing its resolution, and vice versa. Lund gives an example: "When I use my drum scanner on a 35mm slide, I can crop in and scan a portion of it at 5000 dpi [dots per inch, sometimes referred to as ppi, or pixels per inch] and get an RGB file that is .48 by .60 inches in dimension but 20.6 MB in size. If I change the resolution to 300 dpi, the dimensions of that same file become 8 by 10 inches." Most files to be printed on offset presses are set to 300 dpi. Inkjet printers are often set slightly lower. But it's hard to go wrong with 300 dpi at the proper output dimensions.

Lund says he typically scans at a high resolution—usually 1000 dpi but sometimes as high as 5000 dpi, the maximum for his ScanView ScanMate drum scanner. With such a high resolution, it's easy to increase the image dimensions without degrading the image integrity. Imaging experts agree that you never want to increase the resolution of an image in Photoshop (called *interpolation*) because it diminishes image quality. When resizing an image, Lund advises doing so in stepped amounts—say in increments of 10 percent at a time—so you can monitor the image for degradation as you change it.

For those of us not delivering our images to stock agencies—or without a state-of-the-art computer to manage the multimegabyte files—the question remains: If scanning an image, what resolution should you use? For best results, work backwards from the output device, which means asking the print shop that will be printing the final piece about their requirements. If you don't have access to that information, make sure there's 300 dpi for the final output size. If you're scanning a 4 by 5 image that will be printed at 4 by 5, use 300 dpi; but if you're scanning a 4-by-5-inch transparency that will be printed at 8 by 10, that's about 600 dpi.

When resizing images, Lund tends to increase or decrease the document dimensions in increments of 10 percent. (He never increases the resolution.) When the Constrain Proportions option is checked, width and height remain in proportion.

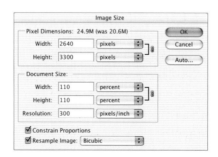

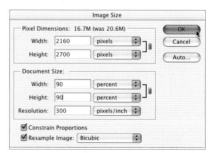

When starting from scratch, set the image size and resolution according to whatever you want your final output to be.

If shooting images with a digital camera, Lund simply captures the scene at the highest resolution the camera can record. As usual, he follows his play-it-safe philosophy: Better to have too much than to find out while you're compositing that you don't have the shot—or the resolution—you need. For those with less computer power, though, the same resolution rules apply for captures from digital cameras. When preparing your digital-camera files for output, the rule of thumb for printing presses is to have 300 dpi at whatever dimensions that output will be. For output to other devices, such as a film recorder, check with the person or company doing the printing for exact requirements.

When you're placing a piece of one image into another file, be aware that the placed image will convert to the resolution of the existing file. When creating a composite, Lund usually uses whatever will be his background image as his original file, so his high-resolution image sets the bar. He notes, though, that if there's a large discrepancy between the resolutions, you may be surprised by the result when you place one image in another. "If you don't like surprises, it's best to set all the parts to the same resolution before starting work," says Lund.

A Finely Tuned Computer

For image processing and compositing, Lund always uses the latest version of Photoshop on the fastest Macintosh he can afford. Lund's Photoshop equivalent of the adage "You can never be too rich or too thin" is "Your computer can never be too fast or have too much RAM." Photoshop will demand as much as your computer can give it. Its requirements change with each new version, so it's impossible to say how much speed and memory you'll need, but as Lund says, "Anyone who is serious about Photoshop spends a lot of money on equipment or else a lot of time twiddling their thumbs."

Not surprisingly for someone who depends on visual feedback to judge his works in progress, Lund calibrates his monitors and color manages his system, using GretagMacbeth equipment.

Getting Down to Work

Opening his background image to begin a composite, Lund sets the Photoshop window mode to Full Screen with Menu Bar. This option places the working image against a nondistracting neutral backdrop. Another benefit of this mode is that, since the entire screen is devoted to Photoshop, an errant click doesn't dump you out onto the desktop or into another program.

Lund usually works with the original canvas size of the background image, and keeps his Photoshop desktop minimal. "About the only palette I keep open all the time is the Layers palette," he says. Everything else is docked until needed.

Now comes the fun part: the "jumping in and doing."

Lund keeps his Photoshop desktop lean and mean: He sets the window to Full Screen Mode with Menu Bar, and displays only the Layers palette until another is needed.

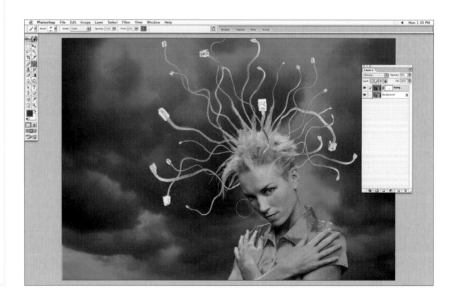

If you had to distill Lund's compositing technique to its essence, it would be: select with the Pen tool, blend with layer masks. You'll see these steps repeated over and over in the chapters that follow. A handful of other tools—not too many—take care of the rest of the work. Many of Photoshop's fancier features, however, are left on the desktop.

Since compositing is basically a process of cutting an image from one photo and placing it in another, Lund has become an expert at selecting complex shapes. His favorite technique—using the Pen tool—is described in Chapter 3, but he'll use others (such as the color-selection tools, describe in Chapter 4), as needed. Photoshop's Pen tool, which operates like the Pen tool in Illustrator, can be labor-intensive on complicated subjects, but Lund swears that the time spent up front is well worth it for the clean selection edges the Pen tool yields. "The best way to learn this incredibly powerful tool is to use it—a lot!" he says, describing the outlining process as a flow of energy, or *ki*. "There's something to be said about relaxing and just going with the 'Zen of the pen.'"

The Pen tool is an indispensable tool for making clean selections in composites.

With the selection pasted into another image, the experimentation starts. Lund experiments with different orientations, brush sizes, colors, opacities, and other settings until each effect looks right to him. His first act with most images is to immediately create a layer mask for the pasted-in selection—using the Hide All option if he wants to paint the image in a bit at a time, or Reveal All if he knows he wants most of the new image showing. He then starts painting the new layer in, bit by bit, usually using soft brushes set to the Airbrush setting for a slow build-up of effect. Soft-edged brushes are better for blending images, while hard-edged brushes are better for defining areas or cleaning up edges, says Lund. He uses a small brush (generally 3 to 20 pixels) for detail work, and large brushes (up to Photoshop's maximum of 2500 pixels) for tasks like masking one image into another. When caught up in creating an image, Lund often just starts with whatever brush size was left over from the operation before.

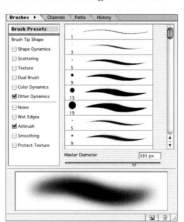

The brush size may vary, but Lund almost always uses a soft-edged airbrush when brushwork is required, especially when painting in images with layer masks.

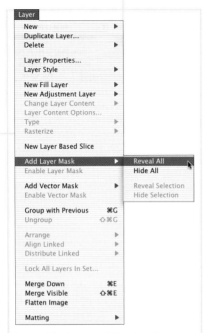

Layer	
New	▶
Duplicate Layer...	
Delete	▶
Layer Properties...	
Layer Style	▶
New Fill Layer	▶
New Adjustment Layer	▶
Change Layer Content	▶
Layer Content Options...	
Type	▶
Rasterize	▶
New Layer Based Slice	
Add Layer Mask	▶
Enable Layer Mask	
Add Vector Mask	▶
Enable Vector Mask	
Group with Previous	⌘G
Ungroup	⇧⌘G
Arrange	▶
Align Linked	▶
Distribute Linked	▶
Lock All Layers In Set...	
Merge Down	⌘E
Merge Visible	⇧⌘E
Flatten Image	
Matting	▶

Reveal All / Hide All / Reveal Selection / Hide Selection

Layer Masks are at the heart of compositing. The Reveal All and Hide All commands set the default state of the layer mask.

Lund admits that he's often care-less in naming his layers—a fact he often regrets later. His original palette for "Pool Dog" (Chapter 14) looked like the one at left until he cleaned it up for the layers illustration in that chapter, shown at right. Naming your layers makes it a lot easier to go back to a par-ticular layer for adjustments.

Layers of Meaning

Layers in general are so critical to Photoshop compositing that it's hard to imagine those brave souls who made composites in earlier eras. As you'll see in the chapters that follow, Lund uses many layers in his composites because they afford him the flexibility to change his mind. His layer philosophy might be summarized as: When in doubt, make a layer. And before you make dramatic changes to a layer, duplicate it first. Make color changes with an adjustment layer instead of alter-ing the entire image. "It's easier to throw away a layer than to make a change to the image that you'll regret later," he says.

Despite his affection for making new layers, Lund admits one failing: He's sloppy about naming layers as he goes. "I get caught up in the flow and don't want to stop. Then later on, I always wish I had named them. I'm trying to correct this, but it's a hard habit to break," he admits. Thankfully, when confused about which layer is which, a keyboard shortcut can save the day: While pressing Command-Option-Ctrl, click on an item to activate the correct layer in the Layers palette.

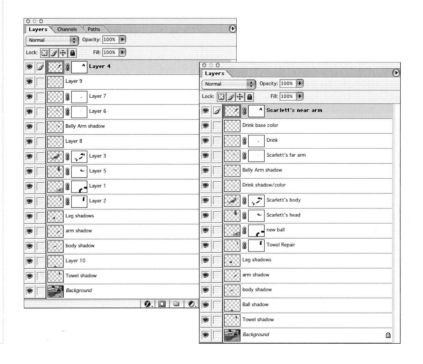

The main thing Lund likes about layers, however, is their masks. For Lund, layer masks are at the heart of compositing and are, he says, "the most fun part."

Adjustment layers are also key to compositing, because with them you can make tonal and color adjustments on a layer-by-layer basis rather than to the entire file. "Every time you make color adjustments, you are throwing away information that will ultimately erode the quality of the image." Lund says, "But with adjustment layers you can make an infinite number of adjustments and readjustments, and not add to the cumulative degradation of the image." And because adjustment layers come with their own layer masks by default, you can adjust just one part of a layer, too.

Fine-Tuning

With the image assembled, Lund turns his attention to the details that will make the image believable as a unified whole. Usually that means attention to the lighting, especially the shadows and highlights.

Lund also checks the edges to see if they need to be softened—abrupt hard edges can give away the fact that an image is a composite. If he sees edges that need adjusting, he uses the Blur tool set at a strength of 100 percent, and with a small brush that just covers the edge in question, softens the edges as needed.

Sharpening is one of the image-correction techniques that most people assume is mandatory. Lund, for one, doesn't think so. As a result there are very few references to sharpening in this book. "I use less sharpening than more," he says. "I'm very conservative about it."

Lund will on occasion sharpen just one area of an image—the eyes for example—and leave the rest untouched. The reason is that the eyes will draw the viewer's attention and give the illusion of sharpness without making the image look grainy or adding the color halos to edges that sharpening can often cause.

Sometimes, sharpening just part of an image is better than sharpening the whole thing, which can produce unwanted color artifacts.

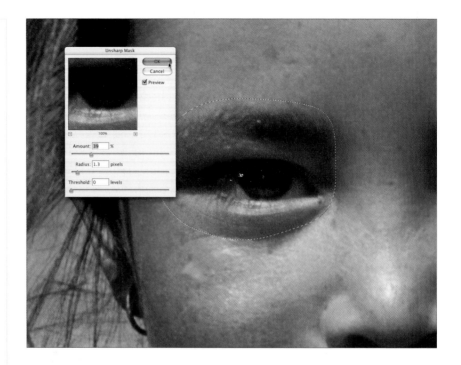

Images from digital cameras are softer than film images and tend to need sharpening. In that case, Lund heeds the advice of a prepress operator who once told him to sharpen the image until it looks just a little too sharpened. "That actually works really well, but again, I always save an unsharpened version, too," Lund says, just in case.

Final Checks and File Preparation

Before sending out a file, Lund performs a number of quality checks. First, he goes to 100-percent view (View> Actual Pixels) and inspects the image. He methodically works his way through every square inch, looking for scanning artifacts, stray pixels, and other aberrations. Then he makes a print. "I often see things in a print that I didn't notice on screen," he says. And whenever time permits, he walks away from the image for a day or two then returns to reassess it. "I get caught up in the excitement of creation. I'm much more objective when I look at it a few days later," he says.

Composites are rife with layers, and any kind of layer adds to the overall file size, so it's always good to flatten the file before you send it out. But be sure to save an unflattened version, too. "I always flatten at the last possible moment," Lund says. "But I keep an unflattened version as a native Photoshop file (indicated by the .psd extension) as well, in case I need to go back to it. If I don't, I guarantee the time will come when I'll need to, and I'll be kicking myself for it."

Most of his clients want CMYK files, but Lund waits until just before sending it out to convert his RGB working files to CMYK. "And then I always keep an RGB version of the file, too," he adds. Lund acknowledges that he always is a bit heartbroken at this stage. "After looking at these deep saturated RGB colors all day, when the screen refreshes to show the

Flattening an image greatly reduces its file size. But always keep a copy with layers intact.

CMYK version, it always looks so different to me. Sometimes I look away until I know the conversion has happened—it's less painful that way," he says. "But CMYK conversion is a fact of life, at least for now."

His most important tool for maintaining color fidelity is to provide his stock agency or prepress house with a color-reference print of the digital file printed on his Epson inkjet. Not all of Lund's clients use color management systems—indeed, some use human color separators—so a good old visual check comparing the file to the reference print may be how color expectations are determined. "Having said that, the color test used for this book was based on ColorSync profiles (no reference print) and were exactly right on when the proofs came back from the printer," Lund adds. Unless specifically told otherwise by a printer, Lund uses the Adobe RGB 1998 color profile for RGB work and the US Sheetfed Coated v2 or US Web Coated (SWOP) V2 profiles for CMYK output.

Now that we have an overall picture of how composites are made, let's zoom in on specific images—with a detailed look at how Lund crafted 12 of his most popular composite images.

Converting RGB files to CMYK should always be done in consultation with your printer, as press requirements vary.

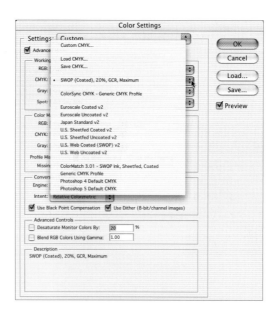

Image by Image

The next chapters each focus on one image and how it was made, with four types of information provided about each one.

The Story

An introduction, in John's words, about why he did the piece and the thinking behind it.

The Parts

The source images John combined to create the final image, with details about how they were shot.

The Process/The Layers

An overview of how the image was created, step by step, describing the Photoshop techniques used for each effect.

At the end, you'll get a view of John's Layers palette, for an inside view of how the image came together.

The Details

A detailed look at how John used an important technique in creating the image. He details each step, along with tips and tricks, for creating an amazing effect with a tool or command that he finds especially useful.

Combining Images

At the heart of Photoshop compositing is the process of combining one image with another. That process can be broken into three steps: selecting the image elements you want to combine, placing them into the base image, and blending the images together. Sounds simple, right? Well, yes and no.

When compositing images, Lund relies on a few tools and a handful of techniques—nothing too fancy or complicated. However, gaining mastery of those tools and techniques takes practice. Lund advocates extensive experimentation, which helps you develop your craft and your eye. You'll be able to determine which methods are appropriate for the situation and discern how extensive your modifications should be. Technique distinguishes a realistic-looking composite from a crude pastiche.

The quest for solid technique is what draws Lund to the Pen tool when he needs to select image elements. Photoshop's Pen tool borrows its Bezier curve and point technology from Adobe Illustrator. You click and drag with the Pen tool around an area, creating control and anchor points along the way. The result is a path that can be saved as a smooth selection. The advantage of this approach is that these points and paths give you precise control over the contours of the selection, but the disadvantage is that making the outline can be time-consuming, especially for users unfamiliar with the Pen tool's seemingly unpredictable behavior. But Lund remains adamant: "The Pen tool is the most important selection tool in Photoshop," he says.

"Often, assistants will apply to work with me. I ask them if they use the Pen tool to make selections, and they almost always say they'd rather use the Magic Wand. And I don't hire them," he says. "All the top photographers use the Pen tool. You can make incredibly precise and totally clean selections with it, and while it takes longer at the outset, you save yourself from the countless hours of cleanup that arise from 'dirty' selections."

That's not to say that Lund never uses other selection tools. For example, Color Range (Select> Color Range), as its name suggests, lets Lund select areas of an image according to a particular range of colors—a

The Pen tool lets you make complex selections that require minimal clean up—if you take the time to do it right.

specific shade of blue, for instance, or all shades of red. Once chosen with Color Range, the selection can be turned into a path, even if the areas are not contiguous. "Color Range is an incredibly versatile selection tool that really saves the day in ticklish situations," Lund notes. "For example, selecting leaves one by one would be madness, but by using Color Range, I can select all the leaves with the same color in one fell swoop."

Lund may disparage the Magic Wand, but he often uses the tool in conjunction with Color Range—for example, when he needs to pick up stray colors that escaped the Color Range operation. "Magic Wand is my least-used selection tool," he admits, "but it can be handy under certain circumstances. If I've made a selection and I spot a small area of a given color that I missed, I use it to grab that color. But to use the Magic Wand well requires a careful eye for spotting the imperfections in a selection."

Alpha channels are also used here as a means of selecting and pasting detailed lines into another image, such as the circuitry showing on the city blocks below.

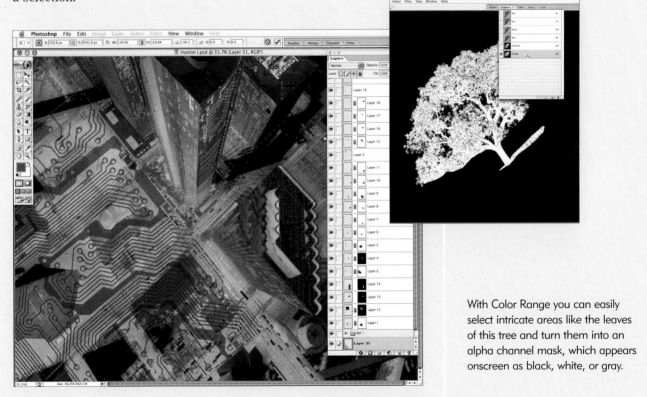

With Color Range you can easily select intricate areas like the leaves of this tree and turn them into an alpha channel mask, which appears onscreen as black, white, or gray.

Alpha channels are another useful tool in Lund' s bag of tricks. "Alpha channels are one of the most difficult concepts to comprehend, but once you do, they open up incredible possibilities," Lund says. Alpha channels let you save complex selections based on a grayscale representation of the image, and as a result can save gradations where dark fades into light, for instance. "You can make amazingly precise selections and store them as an alpha channel to be called up at will and used later." Alpha channels can also be used in combination or with other selections to create highly sophisticated masks.

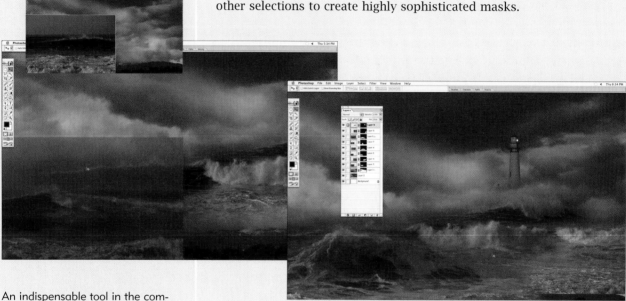

An indispensable tool in the compositor's kit bag is the layer mask, which Lund describes as "painting with images." With layer masks you can make an ocean from single waves.

Whether using the Pen tool, Color Range, or some other device, once the selection is made it has to be placed in the background or base image before they can be blended together. The sequence you'll see Lund use again and again is "copy, paste, position, scale"—although perhaps in a different order, depending on the image. Copy and paste is familiar to anyone who uses a computer. Moving the piece into place can be done with the Move tool. But position and scale require the use of the Transform functions. Lund mostly uses Free Transform (Edit> Free Transform), which puts a bounding box around the placed element. You then use the handles on the bounding box to resize, rotate, or distort the new layer so that it matches the scale and angle of the base image.

Blending one image into another is the essence of compositing, and in Photoshop that means using layer masks. In traditional graphics, a mask is an overlay that protects an image from being painted on or otherwise modified. In Photoshop, a layer mask serves a similar function, but instead of protecting part of an image from change, it controls how much of a layer is visible. You paint in the layer mask to hide or reveal parts of the layer's contents. So if Lund has two ocean waves that he wants to appear as one, for instance, he adds a layer mask to the top wave and paints out bits of the wave until it blends with the bottom wave.

"Layer masks enable me to do what I call 'painting with images,' which I think is an incredibly creative and intuitive way to work," Lund says. "They are absolutely essential to the way I work." Lund can vary the size, shape, and opacity of his paintbrushes to create hard or soft edges where the images join. Once you've mastered the technique, you'll find you use layer masks again and again.

"Layer masks give me the ability to blend images together seamlessly and almost effortlessly," Lund says. "Selections are tedious. Layer masks are fun."

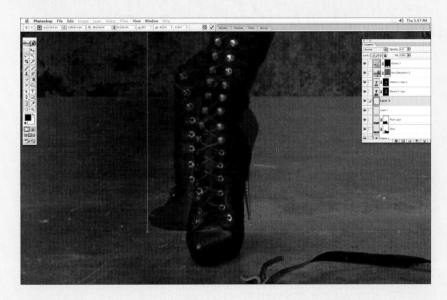

Here, layer masks allow Lund to blend one boot into another to expose an unseen spiked heel.

Featured technique
Pen tool

CHAPTER 3

Making Precise Selections

"The image of a motorcycle gang riding into town and bringing trouble with it has become a worldwide icon. I toyed with, and procrastinated about, doing this shot for a couple of years. I could never figure out where I could get a gang of bikers I'd feel comfortable working with.

One day my ex-brother-in-law Rob had me over to discuss his efforts with Photoshop. There in his driveway was a Harley-Davidson motorcycle. I asked if he knew any biker-looking guys that we could hire for a shoot. He volunteered to ask some Hells Angels he knew. I reluctantly told him to go ahead, even though I was trying to figure out where I could photograph Hells Angels cruising up and down the road. I envisioned permits, lots of model fees, and a pack of very intimidating models—not exactly my style.

Over the next couple of days I began to consider shooting just one or two bikers and using Photoshop to create a gang. I checked with my brother-in-law again. He did have one friend, not a Hells Angel, who he was sure would enjoy doing the shoot for a minimal dollar amount. We were off."

Client: Stock photograph published by Getty Images

Riders

Easy Riders

Rob volunteered to fill in as the second cyclist and scouted a location on a little-used back road, and they were off.

Lund's art director at the stock agency suggested using early-morning light—early morning and late afternoon are optimal times for outdoor photography. But when the morning scheduled for the shoot arrived, so did a dense fog. The fog could be a problem, Lund thought. "I had imagined crisp, clear light and deep-blue sky as a way of bringing out the texture in the image," he says. But on the other hand, he wouldn't have to worry about contrasty lighting, which makes it difficult for film to hold highlights and shadows in the same exposure. The fact that the fog would hide the roadside wasn't important; Lund thought he'd strip in a background of storm clouds to enhance the mood.

Lund and his assistant Sam both lay in the back of a pick-up truck and shot away as the riders took turns following. The photographers used relatively slow shutter speeds, bracketing from one-quarter of a second to one-thirtieth of a second, so that the road would be blurred. Because of the challenges inherent in keeping moving objects in focus, Lund took many shots. The riders kept their speed constant at about 30 miles per hour while swerving back and forth from one side of the pick-up to the other. It took about a dozen passes—and 22 rolls of film—to get all the shots Lund wanted.

Later, back in the studio, Lund was faced with a basic problem: He had only two cyclists, but he needed a gang. In pursuit of variation, he added a moustache to one cyclist, then rustled up a picture of goggles from a file photo that he could use to change another's look. Then he turned to his least expensive model: himself. Sam used a digital camera to capture Lund's face in lighting that approximated the outdoor light on the riders. Lund's face appears on the center rider. "It's only in my fantasies that I get to be a tough guy," Lund says.

The sky is a file shot from a trip he took to Santa Fe, New Mexico.

I can see clearly now: The goggles were shot on Lund's assistant Sam months earlier for an "Animal Antics" composite.

Mug shot: Lund again, looking tough, shot in the studio with a LightPhase digital back mounted on a Hasselblad camera. "I'm a cheap model," he says.

A menacing sky: Storm clouds gathering over Santa Fe, New Mexico.

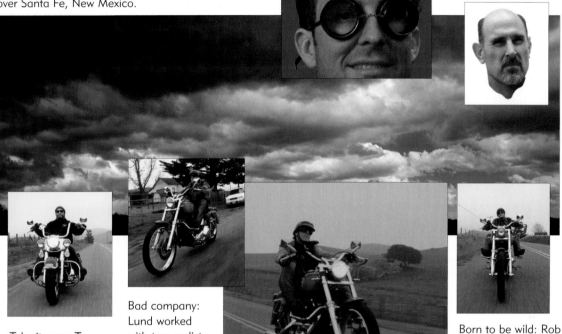

Take it easy: To shoot the motorcycles, Lund and his assistant Sam lay down in the back of a moving pick-up truck.

Bad company: Lund worked with two cyclists, both on Harley-Davidson bikes.

Born to be wild: Rob Nye, Lund's ex-brother-in-law, rode the red bike.

Road kill: Lund forgot to shoot the road without riders, so this frame from the photo shoot was chosen to be the background image (minus the rider, of course).

Down the centerline: Catching the bikes and riders at different angles gave Lund more to work with.

Make way: Lund used Rob's motorcycle for five of the six shots because his extended wheel forks had the "chopper" look he was aiming for.

Head out on that highway: Rob rides again.

Move on Down the Road

He pastes in the clouds and adds a layer mask. With a very large brush, (2000 pixels for this 60-MB file), he paints away unwanted portions of the clouds, merging the image into the background.

The image Lund uses for the background has an unwanted cyclist in it—and unwanted yellow highway markings. "Including the yellow lines would have limited the customer base for the image, because many countries don't have those markings on their roads," Lund says. The new riders will cover up most of the rogue rider and errant lines, but he still needs to remove or hide parts of them. He uses the Polygonal Lasso tool to select some of the roadway and turns that selection into a new layer. Using the Free Transform command, he drags out the bounding box into a shape that covers up the yellow line and hides the lower half of the rider. He also uses the Healing Brush at 945 pixels to strip away most of the rider's body. Lund blends the two layers together with layer masks so that much of the rider and the yellow line disappear. Flattening the image and saving it as "Rider background" completes this step.

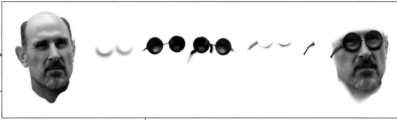

Lund positions his own head in the composite file, then uses a layer mask to erase portions of his face that are hidden by the helmet and the collar of the coat. He then opens the photo that includes the goggles and selects them with the Pen tool. He decides to use the left lens for both lenses because its angle is more in line with that of the face. After he places the left goggle lens, he duplicates that layer, flops it horizontally, and positions the new layer over the right eye. Painting with the airbrush creates shadows under the frames.

Each motorcycle and rider is selected with the Pen tool, copied, then placed, positioned, and sized in the sky file.

To further the illusion of several different riders, Lund varies their apparel. In this case, he turns brown chaps into black ones by selecting the chaps and using the Curves function to darken them.

The careful placing of shadows really makes the image work. To fashion them, Lund creates a new layer for the entire image, selects a large soft-edge brush (1000+ pixels), and paints with one short stroke, starting under the engine of the center rider and moving backwards. With a smaller brush, he paints a single stroke starting just before the center of the tire, where it meets the asphalt. He then uses the Smudge tool to push and pull the shadow into a longer, narrower shape.

Selecting Elements with the Pen Tool

Selecting image components from one photograph and pasting them into another is the foundation of photocompositing. Photoshop gives you several ways to make selections, but the one that Lund uses most is the Pen tool.

Like the Pen tool in Illustrator, Photoshop's Pen tool creates vector paths that are controlled by points. You simply click to create path segments around an object, adding or deleting points as you go. You can have as many points as you like, making the Pen tool the most accurate of Photoshop's selection tools—and also the most labor intensive.

"The trick to using the Pen tool is getting used to its 'sproing' factor," Lund says. "You click on a point, and these long loopy lines spring out at you. It can be quite startling the first time you try it." But once mastered, Lund says, it quickly becomes second nature.

After you draw a path around what you want to select with the Pen tool, the next step is to convert the defined area into a selection. Lund opens the Path palette's menu and clicks Make Selection. This isolates the area of the image you've defined, so you can now add it to other images or place it on other layers within the current image.

"Once you've placed a selection made with the Pen tool, you can relax secure in the knowledge that the selection's edges are artifact free," he says. Such clean edges are important to composites where you want the placed objects to meld seamlessly with other images.

Pen-tooling (as Lund calls it) is so important to his compositing technique—and so mysterious to some Photoshoppers—that we'll go into detail here about its use, with Lund offering tips along the way on how to handle tight spots. Advanced Pen-toolers may want to skip ahead.

Step 1: Creating a curved path with vectors

When it comes to making selections, "It's not so much where you start, it's *that* you start—like in life, getting going is the hardest part," Lund says. He starts by opening the image of the red motorcycle and zooming in to 100% (**Figure 3.1**). He clicks the Pen tool in the Tools palette (**Figure 3.2**), clicks on the Paths option in the bottom bar, then clicks and drags on a point at the top of the helmet but within its inside edge (**Figure 3.3**). "Staying just inside the outline helps eliminate any background from accidentally being included in the selection," Lund says. "It's my natural tendency. As a kid I always stayed inside the lines of my coloring books. Those of you with bumper stickers that say 'Question authority' will have a hard time with this."

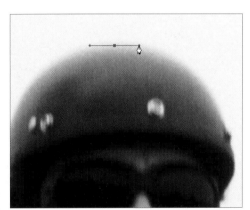

Figure 3.3

Figure 3.1

Figure 3.2

By clicking and dragging, Lund pulls out a handle from the anchor point. "Then I move the mouse to the next location. I click with the Pen tool to create a new anchor point, and a line segment forms between the two points," he says. "Now, while maintaining the pressure on that last click, I drag the Pen tool to make a new handle with which I can align that previous line segment to its proper position." This is how he curves the path behind the new anchor point to follow the helmet's rounded edge (**Figure 3.4**). Dragging a long handle affects the new path segment differently than a short handle would (**Figure 3.5**). If you've never used vector tools before, working with handles and anchor points will feel odd at first, but Lund says you'll quickly get comfortable with it.

"An effective way to learn the Pen tool is to just spend some time creating circles with it," Lund advises. "Once you can create smooth, round circles, you're ready for the big time. You click, you drag, you click, you drag—you can make a circle with 4 points or 400 points, although I don't recommend the latter."

Figure 3.4

Figure 3.5

Step 2: Turning a corner

When Lund comes to a point where he has to make an abrupt change of direction, he clicks and drags. As he drags, a new handle is created, which he uses to align the path segment behind the new anchor point; then he lets go (**Figure 3.6**). Next he holds down the Option/Alt key and adjusts that new handle to influence the subsequent segment in the desired way, which in this case means making a very short handle jutting out approximately 90 degrees from the helmet. By holding the Option/Alt key down while clicking on the new handle, he can move that handle without affecting the previous path segment. He clicks and drags on the next point and uses the handle to adjust the path segment accurately (**Figure 3.7**).

If the leading handle points in the wrong direction for starting the next path segment, Lund holds down the Option/Alt key again and drags the forward handle to a more appropriate angle and length (**Figure 3.8**). He then continues clicking and dragging, keeping the path just inside the edge of the rider's outline.

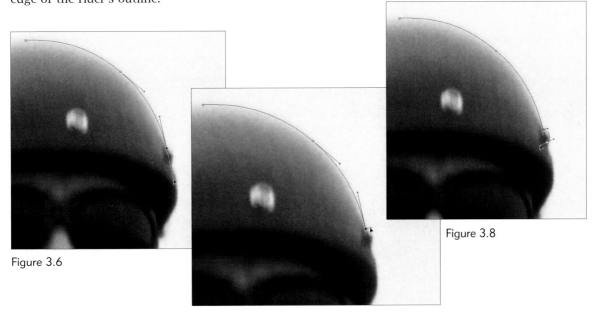

Figure 3.6

Figure 3.7

Figure 3.8

Step 3: Creating a point

At the sharp angle at the rider's coat collar, he simply clicks instead of dragging. This gives him an anchor point with no handles from which the next click will elicit the desired angle (**Figure 3.9**). With that, he is off clicking and dragging again (**Figure 3.10**).

Figure 3.9   Figure 3.10

Step 4: Making it up

When he reaches a point where a defined edge is lost—for example, it's obscured by highlight and chrome—he continues to create the path as he imagines it should be (**Figure 3.11**).

Figure 3.11

Step 5: Correcting mistakes

The nice thing about the paths made with the Pen tool is that, unlike selections made with the Lasso tool, they can be corrected midstream. But Lund would rather avoid that altogether. "I try to be perfect when I make selections because I hate cleaning up later," he says. "You read a lot of Photoshop books where someone says, 'just make a quick outline.' That's not my style. I feel it's a waste of time to clean it up later. Besides, by then I'm already onto the next thing, and cleaning up ruins my creative flow."

If he has to go back and fix a portion of the path, Lund can do one of two things. First, he can hold down the Option/Alt key and click on the anchor point closest to the errant path segment to create two new handles with which to work (**Figure 3.12**). Next, he holds down the Option/Alt key again and clicks and drags on one of the new handles. Then he can adjust the path segments independently of each other (**Figure 3.13**). In the second method, he holds down the Option/Alt key and clicks and drags on the handle of the path until the correction is made (**Figure 3.14**). He then holds down the Option/Alt key again and follows a similar procedure on the other handle to recorrect the path segment behind the controlling anchor point—the one that was misaligned by the act of correcting the forward path segment.

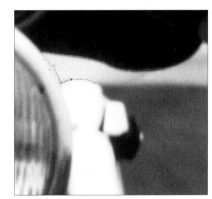

Figure 3.12

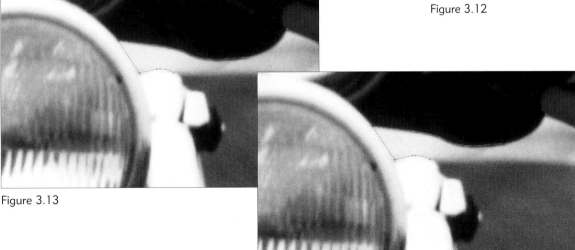

Figure 3.13

Figure 3.14

"Trying to explain this is more difficult than actually doing it," Lund admits. "Just start clicking and dragging, and let osmosis do its work. It'll seep in."

In a case where an anchor point needs to be moved, he holds down the Command/Ctrl key and clicks on the offending anchor point, then drags it to a new location (**Figure 3.15**). If he needs to remove an anchor point, he chooses the Delete Anchor Point tool and clicks on the anchor point he wants to remove (**Figure 3.16**).

Figure 3.15   Figure 3.16

Step 6: Using the Freeform Pen tool

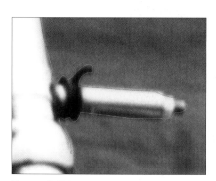

Figure 3.17

In addition to the standard Pen tool, Photoshop offers the Freeform Pen tool, which lets you draw your path and then, instead of placing anchor points as you go, adds them afterwards. Clicking on the Magnetic option makes the Freeform Pen tool create paths automatically by detecting edges based on color, but Lund is seldom satisfied with the results when he uses those tools. "When I use the Freeform Pen tool, I find myself bumping into coffee cups and such with my mouse hand, and that really disrupts things," he says. He prefers the precision of drawing paths by hand; but for making a selection around the cycle's foot pegs, where pinpoint accuracy is less critical, the Freeform Pen tool works just fine (**Figure 3.17**). (Lund wouldn't often change tools midstream, but it's useful to know what each tool does best and then choose accordingly.)

Step 7: Excluding the interior sections

Once he completes the exterior path, Lund uses the Pen tool around interior areas that he wants to exclude from his final selection, such as the interior space of the wheel around the axle (**Figure 3.18**). The finished path is elaborate and riddled with anchor points, but because Lund uses this tool frequently, it didn't actually take him that long to do it. He estimates 10 minutes per motorcycle (**Figure 3.19**). "But after Pen-tooling six motorcyclists, I was ready for a break," he says.

Step 8: Activating the path

Before he can convert the path to a selection, Lund makes sure the entire path is activated, or "live." The path is activated when all its anchor points are visible. When you're finished creating paths, it's not uncommon for a portion of the path to be activated but not all of it. In this image, for instance, Lund needs to activate the path inside the front wheel. To do that, he holds down the Command/Ctrl key and drags the Pen tool over that section (**Figure 3.20**).

Figure 3.18

Figure 3.19

Figure 3.20

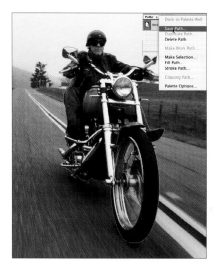

Figure 3.21

Step 9: Saving a path

"At this point I want to save the path, just in case," Lund notes. To do that, he opens the Paths palette. Clicking on the Paths tab shows the Work Path icon (a Work Path is simply an unsaved path). If you click below the icon, you notice that the path disappears from the image—meaning it's deactivated. (Clicking on this icon is another way of activating a deactivated path.)

With the path active, he saves it by choosing Save Path from the Paths palette menu (**Figure 3.21**).

"This is probably a good time to save the entire image, too," says Lund . If I save the path and not the entire file, and the machine crashes before I save the image...guess what? I haven't really saved the path after all."

Step 10: Turning the path into a selection

To turn the path into a new selection, Lund makes sure the path is highlighted in the Paths palette; he then clicks on the upper-right triangle in the Paths palette to open its menu and chooses Make Selection (**Figure 3.22**). Up comes a dialog box that gives him several options. "I choose a feather radius according to the project," Lund says of the Make Selection options. "My default feather radius is usually 1 pixel—and I always click on Anti-alias—but for moving motorcycles I use a 3-pixel feather because the motorcycle has a little movement." (He ended up preferring the shots that were taken at a shutter speed of one-fourth to one-eighth of a second). "You need to match the feather radius to the edge softness of whatever you're selecting," he advises. "The softer the image edge, the larger the feather."

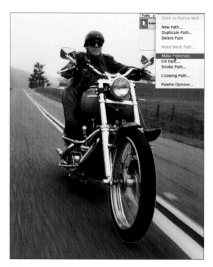

Figure 3.22

Step 11: Pasting in

Lund can now copy this selection and paste the rider into the background file. Using the Free Transform tool (Edit> Free Transform), he rotates, sizes, and positions the rider (**Figure 3.23**) in the image. He uses the same technique five more times to select, copy, and paste riders from other files into the composition to create the final speeding "gang" of bikers.

Lund also makes sure to save versions of the original biker files that include the Pen-tool paths he so laboriously drew. That way, should he ever need a silhouetted biker again, all he has to do is open that version of the image, activate the path, and copy and paste it into a new file. In fact, he did that just the other day when a scene called for a solitary biker.

Figure 3.23

Featured techniques
  Magic Wand
  Color Range
  Background Eraser
  Alpha channels

CHAPTER 4

Making Complex Selections with Color Tools

"Siri Stafford, my art director at Getty Images, suggested the idea of an image showing lightning striking a tree. It's a great concept, but what the heck would it really look like?

To get some ideas, I turned to that technological development that has so radically changed the world of commercial photography: the Internet. I went to Google's image search and typed in 'lightning and tree.' In just a few minutes I had found some obviously amateur images that were nonetheless stunning, actual images of lightning hitting trees. Now I had something to aim for.

In my mind I pictured a lonely expanse of land with a single oak tree. The sky is dark from storm clouds, the time is dusk. A lightning bolt hits the tree and lights up the scene around it. The bolt travels down the trunk of the tree, illuminating the leaves from both above and behind at the same time.

Just a few days before writing this, I received an email from a calendar company who found this image on my Web site," says Lund. "They wanted to know the details of where and how I had captured this image, as well as reassurance that I had not 'enhanced it' digitally!"

Client: Stock photograph for Getty Images

Lightning Strike

Lightning Strikes Twice

There are lots of oak trees near Lund's home in Marin County, California. Scouting an open space nearby, he found one that suited his needs. He photographed it just before noon with a slight backlighting. "My thinking went like this: If a tree was really illuminated by a lightning bolt, then the light would be directly overhead—just as it is at noon," Lund says. He used a Hasselblad 2¼-inch medium-format camera for this shot. Because of the tree's size, shape, and location, Lund had to shoot it on the diagonal, to get it all in the frame.

In the same area, he found and photographed an open expanse of land with a foreground of wild oats. From his files he found a photo of another landscape with low hills in the background and a shot of cloudy skies.

That left the lightning. During a recent winter trip to Ladakh, a region in India often referred to as 'Little Tibet,' he had gotten the shot he used now. "It was long after dark and I was suffering both from altitude sickness and a bout of the flu, exacerbated by the extreme cold in my unheated guest room," Lund remembers. A flash of light lit up the room, and an immediate rush of thunder testified to the closeness of the storm. Here was his chance. "With my head spinning, I groggily shoved a roll of film in my Nikon F100, steadied it on the windowsill, opened the shutter, and waited. Boom! Another flash. I repeated the procedure until I had shot a roll, then climbed, shaking, back into my cot." That effort paid off, he thought, as he scanned in the lightning photo for "Lightning Strike."

Siri Stafford oversaw the compositing of this image. "It involved a tremendous amount of experimentation," Lund remembers. "Given that I was working with 100-megabyte-plus files, it also took a lot of time—a week or so to get it right." At one point, Lund thought he was done, but when he woke up the next morning, the lightning didn't look quite right to him; so he got back to work.

A dark and stormy night: The lightning was photographed during a spectacular nighttime storm in the Ladakh region of India in the Himalayas.

Dark clouds above: An ominous sky hangs over Santa Fe, New Mexico. Lund photographed it with his Fuji Panorama camera.

California pastoral: Lund photographed the grasslands near his house in Northern California with a Hasselblad 2¼-inch camera.

From little acorns: The oak tree sits in a field near where the grasslands were photographed. He searched for a solitary oak tree so that it would be easier to silhouette in Photoshop.

Lightning in a Bottle

With its abundant foliage, the tree is too complex to select using the Pen tool, so instead Lund turns to a trio of tools: Color Range, Magic Wand, and Lasso. With these he makes three separate alpha channels—one each for the leaves, the trunk, and the limbs with the remaining foliage.

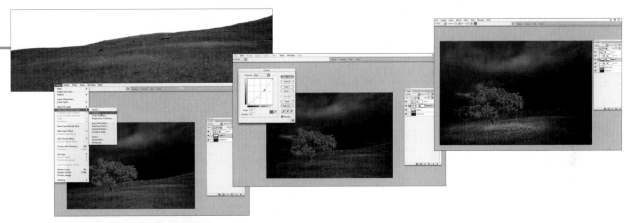

Lund strips the sky out from behind the grassy hill by using the Background Eraser. He then pastes the rolling field as a new layer into the main image, making sure it's positioned beneath the tree layers in the Layers palette. He duplicates that field layer, and applies a Curves Adjustment layer to darken it. He blends the original and darkened layers together using layer masks. By doing so, he can bring up the lightness around the base of the trunk so that the ground looks like it's lit by lightning. He continues working in this fashion, lightening and brightening some areas of the ground and the tree with Brightness/Contrast and darkening others with Curves until he gets the visual mood he wants.

Lund heightens the drama of the lightning bolt by pasting it in with the Layers property set to Lighten. He rotates it into place, then creates an adjustment layer and uses Curves to darken the image enough to eliminate all but the lightning bolt itself. He uses the Liquify brush to fine-tune the path of the bolt.

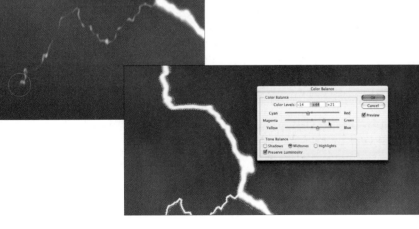

The forks and branches of lightning in the sky are brightened using the Dodge tool. Lund adds a layer and paints over the lightning tendrils with an airbrush to make them show up better. He then selects the lightning with the Magic Wand, creates a new layer, and gives the selection a 12-pixel feather. He creates a glow around the lightning bolt by filling this selection with white. By shuffling the order of layers and working with layer masks, he weaves the lightning through the leaves and down the trunk of the tree.

Making Selections with Color Range and the Magic Wand

You've seen how Lund uses Photoshop's Pen tool to select precise shapes. Another way that Lund selects areas of an image is to use Photoshop's color-selection tools: the Magic Wand and the Color Range command. Instead of following an outline, as with the Pen tool, or grabbing a large area, as with a Marquee or Lasso, color-selection tools let you choose areas based on the colors (more exactly, the brightness of the pixels) they contain. So if you want to select a red barn that's set against a blue sky, Photoshop can analyze the color data in the image and select just the red pixels of the barn, leaving the blue sky untouched.

The color-selection tools are especially powerful in images with a lot of detail. For example, in "Lightning Strike," individually selecting the leaves of an oak tree with the Pen tool would be mind- and wrist-numbing, if not impossible. But the color-selection tools make quick work of it.

With the Magic Wand, you click the color you want to select; the Magic Wand then selects colors with the same values (within a specified tolerance range). Lund mostly uses the Magic Wand when he wants to select color in a specific area of the image or to pick up stray colors not included in other selection operations. Toggling the Contiguous option on and off determines whether the Magic Wand confines its selection to one area or selects all image colors in that range.

Color Range (Select> Color Range) also bases its selection on image color data, but it works differently than the Magic Wand. "I really prefer to use Color Range when possible," Lund says. "Magic Wand is simple—a pixel is either selected or it's not. Color Range lets you make selections according to degrees of color intensity, which I find much more flexible, precise, and useful."

With Color Range, you sample the color you want to select with the built-in Eyedropper, and Color Range looks at the entire image (or within a marqueed selection) for all instances of that color, no matter how dispersed it is in the image. You can expand the range of colors chosen by increasing the Fuzziness value. The plus and minus Eyedroppers let you add and subtract the color to and from a selection. For images with a lot of detail and distributed colors, Color Range is the way to go, Lund says.

In "Lightning Strike," Lund uses both the Magic Wand and Color Range to make complex selections of lightning bolts and tree leaves. He also introduces the concept of alpha channels, which he'll explore more in the next chapter. Plus, he employs another tool that works by sensing clicked-on colors: the Background Eraser, which wipes out pixels that match sampled colors, replacing them with transparency.

Step 1: Isolating the grass with the Background Eraser

Lund opens the sky image (which he'll use as the background) and then the grassland image, the source of the hill he'll put under the tree. He increases the sky image's canvas size to give himself room to add the grass. He also picks the "full screen with menu" option from the toolbox. ("That way, if I accidentally click outside of the image area, I don't end-up bumping myself out of Photoshop and onto the Mac Desktop," he says.)

In the grassland image, his first step is to strip out the hills and sky above the grass with the Background Eraser tool. Initially, he sets the Background Eraser's Limits option to Contiguous, and he sets Tolerance (the range of color selected) to 10%. He then chooses a small soft brush (90 pixels for this 60 MB file) (**Figure 4.1**).

Figure 4.1

He clicks on the dark area above the grass to set the colors the Background Eraser will remove and starts dragging the brush across the line where the foreground and background meet (**Figure 4.2**). He experiments with different size brushes and greater degrees of tolerance until he gets the desired effect along the top edge of the grass (**Figure 4.3**)—erasing just the pixels in the background and not those that make up the hill. "With a large brush, the erasing effect will be more gradated, especially near the edges," Lund explains. "With a smaller brush, the result will be more opaque."

When he thinks he's got the hill isolated, he zooms out to see the whole image, then uses the Lasso tool to select the remaining chunk of sky and delete it (**Figure 4.4**). With everything gone but the grass, he can now simply copy and paste the grass image into the sky image and use Free Transform to size it appropriately (**Figure 4.5**).

Figure 4.2

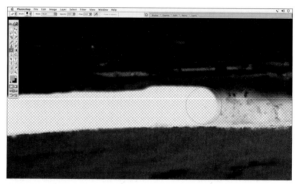

Figure 4.3

Figure 4.4

Figure 4.5

Step 2: Selecting the tree's canopy with Color Range

Now Lund wants to add the tree to the composite image. Though he almost always reaches first for his trusty Pen tool, he knows that, given the tree's intricate shape, using it in this case would be, in his word, insane. Selecting the complex colors and shapes of the tree will call for both the Magic Wand tool and the Color Range command, with help from most of the other selection tools on the palette. Lund's technique will be a roundabout one: selecting everything in the image that's *not* the tree, and then inverting the selection.

"It struck me as simpler to select the blue background than to select the many shades of green in the tree's foliage. When the sky selection is inverted, all the leaves are selected," Lund says. Lund will then make three separate alpha channels—one for the main tree, one for the leaf canopy, and a third for the trunk and limbs—that he will then combine to create the final selection.

He opens the tree image (**Figure 4.6**), then chooses Select> Color Range. "I did a quick test using both the Magic Wand and Color Range, and determined that Color Range was faster and better," Lund says. "When in doubt, pick up a tool and try it. You'll know pretty quickly which one suits your style."

Figure 4.6

The Color Range dialog box opens and the pointer turns into an Eye-dropper. In the Color Range dialog box, Lund sets the Fuzziness to 33, which extends its reach into adjacent pixels of similar tone, and then uses the Color Range eyedropper to click on the blue sky. He Shift-clicks at other points in the sky to get the whole range of blue values (**Figure 4.7**). "I now zoom *waaaay* in," says Lund (675%) until he sees individual pixels and Shift-clicks on any blue or purple pixels he sees (**Figure 4.8**). He monitors his progress in the Preview window in the Color Range dialog box.

Figure 4.7

Figure 4.8

When all the sky pixels are selected, he inverts the selection (Select> Inverse). Now the sky is removed from the selection, but he still needs to get rid of unnecessary objects. With the Lasso tool (1-pixel feather), he holds the Option/Alt key down to deselect the trees on either side of the main tree, the trunk of the main tree, and the foreground grass. (Holding down the Option/Alt key subtracts from selections.) Now only the foliage of the main tree is selected.

Not selecting the tree trunk in this step was a deliberate decision. "This was such a complex selection to do that I felt more comfortable tackling one aspect at a time. I did the leaves first, and then the trunk." Lund says. "It's OK to break it down, and in fact that approach can give you more control than trying to do it all at once."

Step 3: Creating and cleaning an alpha channel

Lund now wants to save this complex selection as an alpha channel (Select> Save Selection). If he didn't save it, all that work of singling out the leaves would be lost. An *alpha channel* is a grayscale version of an image that's stored alongside the color channels (for instance, red, green, and blue) that make up an image. Lund views alpha channels as the most accurate way to save a selection. Another advantage to alpha channels is that he can edit them by applying image adjustments, painting on them, and so on.

He names the resulting channel Tree One (**Figure 4.9**), then opens that channel (Window> Channel), making sure the Tree One channel is selected. He deselects the current selection (Select> Deselect). Then at 100% magnification he uses Threshold (Image> Adjustments> Threshold) to edit the alpha channel, moving the slider to the right until virtually all the white specks in the sky area—snippets of stray color that escaped the selection process—disappear (**Figure 4.10**). Because the mask appears in black and white, it's much easier to see the white artifacts, which were difficult to see in the image itself.

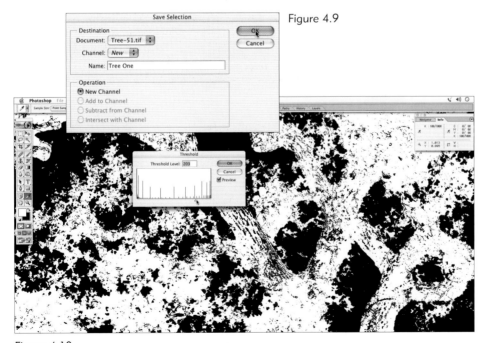

Figure 4.9

Figure 4.10

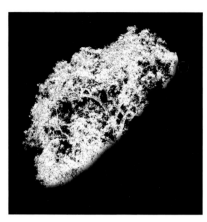

Figure 4.11

Step 4: Softening the selection

"Edges of objects in the real world seldom appear totally sharp to us, so I want to soften the edges of the selected leaf canopy," Lund says. Lund gives the channel a 0.8-pixel Gaussian Blur (Filter> Blur> Gaussian Blur). He then completes the effect by brushing along the bottom edge of the foliage with a 400-pixel brush (**Figure 4.11).**

Step 5: Selecting the tree trunk with the Magic Wand

Lund's next addition to the image will be the trunk and limbs of the tree. "As much as I love the Pen tool, there are times when it's just not the right thing to use," Lund says. "For example, the bark on the tree trunk is gnarly and clumpy—another area that would be tedious to select with the Pen tool."

Still in the tree image, he leaves the alpha channel and goes back to the RGB channel (Command/Ctrl-~). He chooses the Magic Wand. He selects settings (Tolerance: 32, Anti-aliased: checked, Contiguous: unchecked) that allow him to choose color only in a specific area—in this case the trunk and limbs—rather than across the entire image.
With the Magic Wand pointer, he selects several spots on the tree's trunk, Shift-clicking to add to the selection (**Figure 4.12**), until all of its colors are selected, but no sky is included.

Figure 4.12

"The Magic Wand gets into all those jagged little edges—but it also picks up some of the surrounding areas that have similar colors," Lund notes. He isn't concerned that the leaves are included—those will be in the final image anyway—but the grassy area needs to be removed.

Step 6: Eliminating the Background

To eliminate the miscellaneous grass, background trees, and other things included in the current selection, Lund returns to the Pen tool. "I use the Pen tool to draw a wide swath around the area that I want to deselect," he says.

So with the Pen tool he draws a path around the outside of the tree trunk, including all of the grassy areas and other trees that he doesn't want in the final image. He will use this path to eliminate those elements (**Figure 4.13**). Why the Pen tool when a Lasso selection will accomplish the same thing? "It's really a matter of personal style," Lund says. "I feel really comfortable with the Pen tool, so I can draw the line pretty quickly—and it doesn't need to be exact in this situation: The important outlines are already defined. Plus, the Pen tool is more forgiving. If you make a mistake with the Pen tool, you can correct the path without having to start all over again. Not so with the Lasso. If I goof up with the Lasso, it's Command-Z, do it again."

Figure 4.13

He converts the Pen-tool path to a selection (Paths palette menu> Make Selection), choosing Anti-aliased, 1-pixel feather, and Subtract from Selection as his options (**Figure 4.14**). Because he's using the Subtract from Selection option, he is in fact deselecting, or removing, the selected elements from the currently selected area. Now the selection consists of the tree, which he saves as an alpha channel (Select> Save Selection) and names Trunk. Then, clicking on the Trunk channel in the Channels palette (**Figure 4.15**), he blurs it with a 0.8-pixel Gaussian Blur (Filter> Blur> Gaussian Blur).

Command/Ctrl-~ returns him to the main image in the RGB-composite channel.

Step 7: Loading the selections

Now he finishes the process of selecting the tree, with all its thick foliage, twisted limbs, and bumpy bark intact. This involves cleaning up the alpha channels and loading them as selections.

Figure 4.14

Figure 4.15

With the Magic Wand (Tolerance: 32, and with Anti-aliased and Contiguous both checked), Lund selects and Shift-clicks various leaves on the lower part of the tree—leaves that should have been selected earlier but were not (**Figure 4.16**). He saves this selection as an alpha channel named Leaves. Command/Ctrl-6 takes him to that channel.

In the Leaves alpha channel, he paints the trunk black with a 400-pixel brush (**Figure 4.17**). Remember that an alpha channel is a grayscale representation of the image; therefore, painting with black on the trunk protects, or masks, that area (this will be clearer when we talk about layer masks in Chapter 6). Once again, he gives this channel a 0.8-pixel Gaussian Blur (**Figure 4.18**).

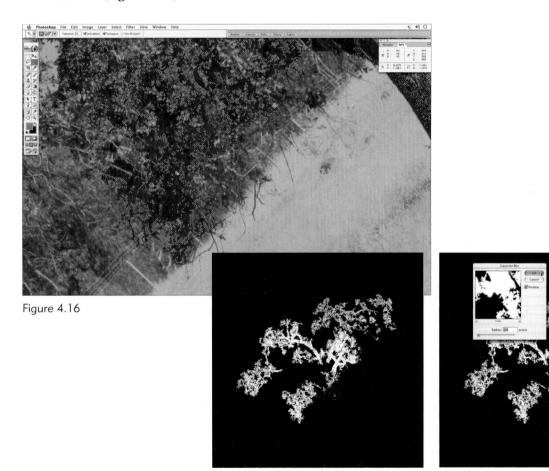

Figure 4.16

Figure 4.17

Figure 4.18

Command/Ctrl-~ takes him back to the RGB channel. He loads the channel called Tree One (Select> Load Selection) with the Add to Selection button chosen in the dialog box (**Figure 4.19**). In the same way, he loads the Leaves channel and the Trunk channel. He now has one saved selection (alpha channel) that includes the entire tree. "The alpha channels have now done their work," Lund says. "I have used them to create a very thorough and precise selection of the tree."

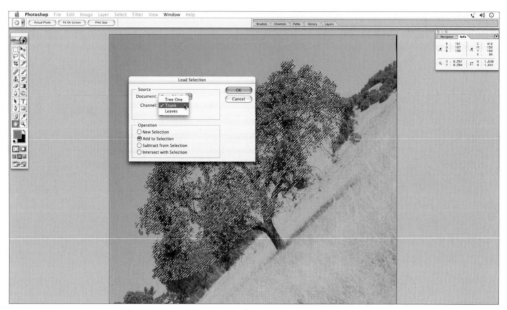

Figure 4.19

Step 8: Placing the tree

Zooming in to 100%, Lund finds a few leaves here and there that need to be added to the combined tree selection, which he does with the Lasso tool set at a 1-pixel feather. To eliminate any fringed edges that may appear when pasting the tree into the composite, Lund goes to Select> Modify> Contract to shrink the selection by 2 pixels (**Figures 4.20** and **4.21**). Now he simply copies and pastes the tree into the main image (**Figure 4.22**). Command/Ctrl-T brings up the Transform tool, which he uses to rotate, size, and position the tree layer. Now that the tree is situated in the landscape, Lund can turn to the task of adding the lightning.

"For an image like this, there is no magic bullet," Lund concedes. "It's tedious and exacting work, but it needs to be done." The result is striking.

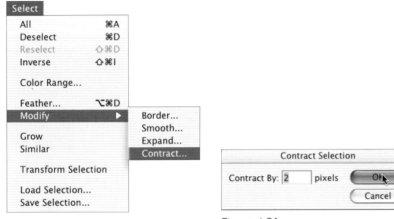

Figure 4.20

Figure 4.21

Figure 4.22

Featured techniques
Transform with Distort
Alpha channels

CHAPTER 5

Tricks for Pasting Images into New Environments

"I was in an art store and picked up a catalog. On the cover was an illustration of a city viewed from above with an extreme wide-angle perspective. Some of the buildings, if my memory serves me, were actually computer chips. One thing that struck me about the image was how similar it was to a photograph I had taken from a helicopter above Houston. With Photoshop I could actually take this borrowed idea even further by adding the element of photographic reality. Such an image could represent the future, technology, the Internet—all kinds of concepts, really. I was inspired to expand on this concept and add something unique to it.

With this in mind I unearthed the transparency of Houston and scanned it. I sat in front of the screen pondering what to do first. More out of curiosity than anything else, I hit Command-I to invert the image. A cool thing happened: The day shot of Houston became night. I played with the curves to fine-tune the nighttime effect. It looked like lights from the street were illuminating the lower portions of the tall buildings. I shot some circuit boards I had around, and added them to the buildings and streets, and I had an image."

Houston, We Have a Photo

The aerial shot of Houston came about during an assignment for DHL, the courier and transport company. Lund was hired to photograph its facilities across the country: New York, Chicago, Los Angeles, Houston, and so on. Some of these city photos have appeared in other Lund composites.

The photos were taken from a helicopter, with Lund leaning out of an open doorway and taking shots looking straight down. "When doing aerial shoots, the helicopter goes in tight spins over the area to be photographed. It's a bit disorienting," Lund says. "As long as I'm looking through my camera, I'm OK; but when I'm not, I get a little woozy."

The circuit boards came from computers Lund has used—and dismantled—over the years. He could have used the same board over and over, but he wanted the variety of line and pattern that different circuitry offered. "I always keep stuff like this around," he says. "I just knew that one day I'd need them for a high-tech picture—like this one."

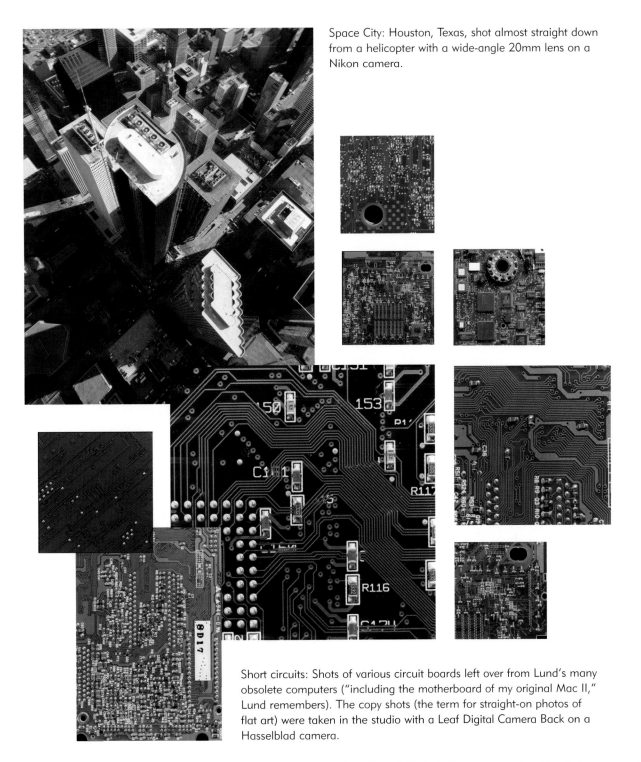

Space City: Houston, Texas, shot almost straight down from a helicopter with a wide-angle 20mm lens on a Nikon camera.

Short circuits: Shots of various circuit boards left over from Lund's many obsolete computers ("including the motherboard of my original Mac II," Lund remembers). The copy shots (the term for straight-on photos of flat art) were taken in the studio with a Leaf Digital Camera Back on a Hasselblad camera.

Bright Lights, Big City

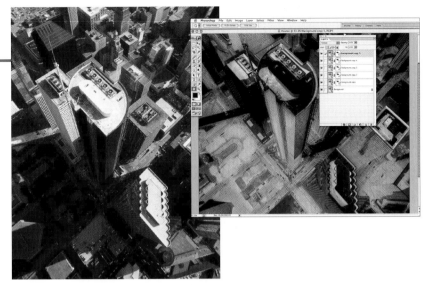

Lund uses the Invert command to reverse the colors in the photo of Houston, then duplicates that layer in Multiply mode, which darkens it further. He adds a layer mask to prevent the lighter roofs from being affected, and then duplicates that new layer and mask in Multiply mode several more times. The net effect: the city at night.

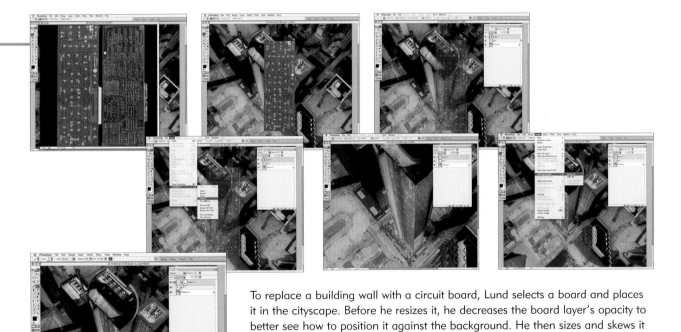

To replace a building wall with a circuit board, Lund selects a board and places it in the cityscape. Before he resizes it, he decreases the board layer's opacity to better see how to position it against the background. He then sizes and skews it with Transform's Distort command, so that it maps to the shape of the building. With a layer mask and a large soft-edge brush, he paints away the bottom of the circuit board, thus allowing more of the underlying building to show through.

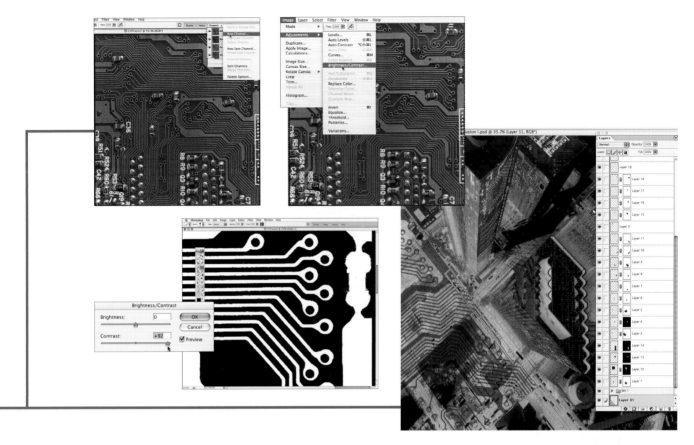

To simulate the light on the street from the headlights and taillights of passing cars, Lund uses a series of Pen-tool paths stroked with yellow and red.

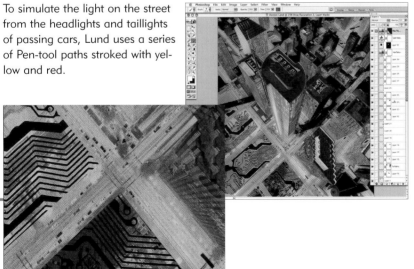

To add an electronic texture to the buildings, Lund makes a mask out of the circuit board's electronic traces using alpha channels. He increases the contrast of the selection in order to isolate the lines on the circuit board, then cleans up the mask by painting with a hard-edged brush on the respective black and white areas. He returns to the RGB channel, loads the selection, copies it, and returns to the main image. He can now paste the traces as a new layer into the city image and use Free Transform to position and size the new layer.

THE LAYERS

How the image stacks up

The red hue—the city must be heating up—comes from a Hue/Saturation adjustment layer set to Colorize. Lund uses a layer mask to paint the red into the lower left.

Putting Objects in Place Using Distort and Alpha Channels

After selecting the image elements, the next step is placing them into the composite image. Copying and placing via your computer clipboard is an essential part of this process, but just pasting one image into another will rarely give you the effect you want. This section covers two techniques that help the new piece fit into its new surroundings.

Photoshop's Transform operations—such as Scale, Rotate, Skew, Distort, and Flip—let you shape the new piece in an appropriate size and orientation. You've already seen Lund use Free Transform (Command/Ctrl-T), which allows you to apply multiple transformations with a single command by clicking on different handles and holding down different modifier keys. In "Circuit City," he uses a specific method of transformation—Distort—to align circuit boards to building facades. Lund forsakes his usual Free Transform tool here for Distort because it allows him to move each corner point independently.

You've also already seen Lund use alpha channels, when he used them to store a complex selection in "Lightning Strike." Here in "Circuit City," alpha channels play a similar role but with a twist: Lund uses them to make part of an image transparent, so that only the parts he wants to show appear in the new environment.

Mapping Images onto Surfaces with Distort

After turning day into night by using the Invert command (Image> Adjustments> Invert) and by repeatedly applying the Multiply layer mode (**Figure 5.1**), Lund now alters the face of Houston. His plan is to map the circuit boards onto the vertical planes of the buildings. The challenge is that the buildings were photographed from above, giving the walls a skewed perspective. The circuit boards, on the other hand, are rectangular with nice square corners.

To remedy this, he uses Edit> Transform> Distort (**Figure 5.2**), which lets him adjust a selection's dimensions and angles by tugging on its handles or side segments. Distort is more flexible than Skew because it operates not just on one side, but also on adjacent sides, giving the effect of stretching the selection.

Figure 5.1

Figure 5.2

Step 1: Distorting to fit

Lund uses the Polygonal Lasso tool to select one of the circuit boards (**Figure 5.3**), then copies and pastes it into the Houston image. First giving the new circuit-board layer an opacity of 50% so he can see the underlying shape, he selects Edit> Transform> Distort (**Figure 5.4**). When handles appear at each corner of the layer, he drags each corner so that the circuit board layer matches the shape and perspective of the building (**Figure 5.5**), then hits Return.

Figure 5.5

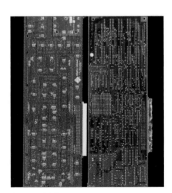

Figure 5.3

Figure 5.4

"Distort is a powerful tool that's simple to use," Lund says. "All I really have to do is match the corner handles of the boards to the corner points of the building, and the board stretches to fit the spaces. I zoom in and examine the lines, fine-tuning the angles until I get the right perspective."

He then sets the board's opacity to 75%—not for image placement but because he wants the board to be more visible while allowing some of the texture of the underlying building to show through.

Step 2: Trimming to size

Even after distorting the circuit board, its shape doesn't map exactly to the shape of the building. Lund sees that he needs to trim the excess.

"To get an accurate fit to the walls, I'll use the Pen tool on many if not most of the buildings," he says. "That way I can make selections from those paths and use them to delete the portions of the circuit boards that extend beyond the edges."

After drawing around the building with the Pen tool, he converts the resulting path to a selection (**Figure 5.6**), inverts that selection (Select> Inverse), and presses the Delete/Backspace key to delete anything outside those edges on the layer. Now the circuit board is an exact fit.

With Command/Ctrl-D, he deselcts the current selection. Then he adds a layer mask (Layer> Add Layer Mask> Reveal All), and, with a large, soft brush and the foreground set to black, paints away the bottom of the circuit board to make it look like it's lit from below (**Figure 5.7**).

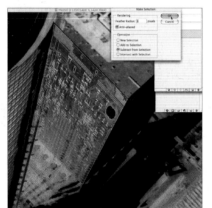

Figure 5.6

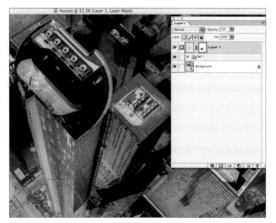

Figure 5.7

This process of selecting the boards, pasting them in, distorting, trimming, and masking them, and then fading the lower portions continues until most of the buildings sport circuit boards.

Step 3: Cutting corners

The tall building in the center—with its curved façade, multilevel roof, and antenna—poses a special challenge, requiring a bit more finesse. First Lund wraps a circuit board around the curved surface of the building using a combination of the Liquify brush (Filter> Liquify) to warp the board (**Figure 5.8**), Skew (Edit> Transform> Skew) to line up the edges of the circuit board with those of the building (**Figure 5.9**), and Distort (Edit> Transform> Distort) for final positioning (**Figure 5.10**).

Figure 5.8

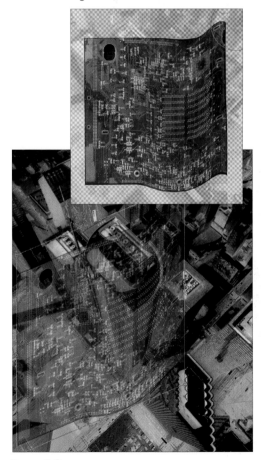

Figure 5.10

Figure 5.9

Using the Pen-tool path he already made of the building to trim the circuit boards, he inverts the selection he made and then presses the Delete key. This removes the excess board outside the building path (**Figure 5.11**).

Toward the end of the process, he also adds a circuit pattern to the oval structure on the main roof—outlining the area with the Pen tool, converting the path to a selection with a 1-pixel feather, pasting a board layer into the selection (Edit> Paste Into), and using Free Transform to size and position the new board (**Figure 5.12**). He's now done applying circuit boards to the cityscape.

Figure 5.11

Figure 5.12

Masking Images onto Surfaces
with Alpha Channels

The buildings now electrified, Lund turns his attention to the streets below. The challenge here is different—not fitting the image into an irregular shape, but rather placing it so that it doesn't obscure everything behind it. That's a job for alpha channels.

What is an alpha channel exactly? All Photoshop images are composed of three channels of data, one for each color: red, green, and blue (**Figure 5.13**). (The RGB channel combines all three.) An alpha channel is an additional track of image data that contains information not about color but about transparency and opacity. When you save a selection as an alpha channel, you can then use the alpha channel as a mask either to protect images areas from, or to expose images areas to, manipulation. Alpha channels store data about transparency as well as shape, so masks made with alpha channels can also expose or hide image data to different degrees in different areas.

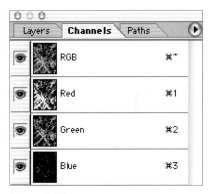

Figure 5.13

When you view an alpha channel, you see a grayscale representation of your selection: black indicates protected areas, white indicates exposed areas, and gray indicates areas that are semitransparent. (A good rule of thumb, Lund notes, is "Black hides all, white reveals all.")

For "Circuit City," Lund wants the city to seem filled with moving information. To do this, he'll use alpha channels to isolate traces from circuit boards (*traces* are the paths on the circuit that the electricity follows) and integrate them into the city scene by placing only the circuitry onto the city blocks.

Step 1: Bringing the street into view
Before he can make the alpha channel, Lund needs to lighten the streets; they're the light source that illuminates the bottom of the buildings. Lightening the streets will also help him see what he's doing when he places the traces on top of them.

Lund returns to the background layer and inverts it again (Select> Inverse) and turns off Layer Set 1, which holds the Multiply layers that he used to darken the image back in the beginning of the composite process. Now he can more clearly see the street area at the bottom of the image.

Step 2: Pen-tooling the blocks

As he did with the buildings, Lund draws paths around the city blocks with the Pen tool (**Figure 5.14**). These paths, too, will be turned into selections that he'll use to trim extra material from the city blocks. He does this to leave the streets clear so he can later insert the stroked paths that mimic electric current.

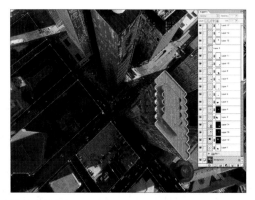

Figure 5.14

Step 3: Creating an alpha channel

Lund now opens the traces file ("one of the circuit boards that boasted some particularly nice-looking circuitry," Lund notes), selects the image (Command/Ctrl-A), and copies it. He uses Channels palette menu> New Channel to create a new channel and then pastes the copied image into it (**Figures 5.15** and **5.16**). He's just created an alpha channel, which appears as a grayscale rendition of the selection.

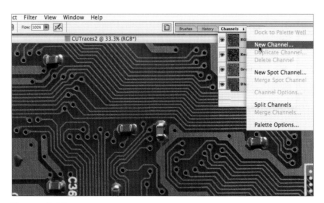

Figure 5.15

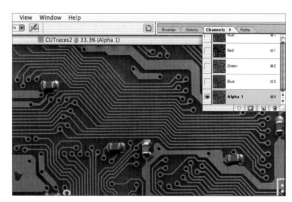

Figure 5.16

To make the traces fully opaque, Lund increases the channel's Contrast to 100% (Image> Adjustments> Brightness/Contrast) (**Figure 5.17**). Now the alpha channel of the labyrinthine traces includes only black and white, with black representing opaque areas and white representing transparent areas (**Figure 5.18**). When the alpha channel is loaded—which creates a selection—only the traces will be selected and then pasted into the image—not the green background.

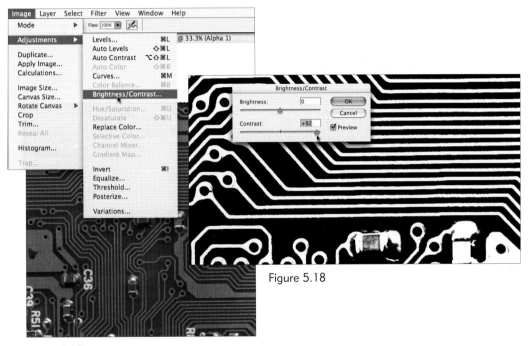

Figure 5.18

Figure 5.17

Given Lund's fondness for the Pen tool and the relative simplicity of the traces pattern (especially when compared with the complexity of other objects he's Pen-tooled), why didn't he just directly select the traces with the Pen tool? Lund explains: "What makes this suited for an alpha channel is the makeup of the circuit board—complex lines with good contrast. There's a lot of contrast between the silver traces and green board, so the two colors are easy to separate into black and white using the Brightness/Contrast control. Once in a while, there's actually something that works better than the Pen tool."

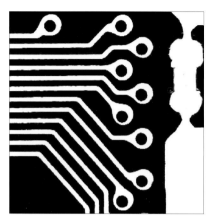

Figure 5.19

Step 4: Cleaning up the mask

"After the Brightness/Contrast step, I've got a pretty good mask, but I want to clean it up," Lund says. He wants the alpha channel mask to have sharp, uninterrupted edges.

Using a hard-edged paintbrush, he cleans up the line edges, zooming in and painting with black on the black, opaque areas and with white on the white, transparent areas. He's looking for wobbly lines or stray pixels that might affect the look of the traces as they show through the white areas (**Figure 5.19**). He also deletes any parts of the circuit board mask that aren't a trace.

Step 5: Applying the alpha channel

The clean and tidy alpha channel of the traces will now be turned into a selection, which means that, when copied, only the traces will be pasted into the city image. To do this, Lund selects the RGB channel in the Channels palette (to display the full-color image), then loads the selection (Select> Load Selection) (**Figure 5.20**). He copies it (**Figure 5.21**), goes back to the city image, and pastes the selection in.

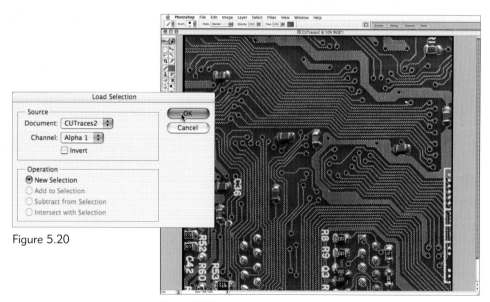

Figure 5.20

Figure 5.21

Step 6: Distorting and trimming to fit

He rotates the board with Free Transform. Then, with Edit> Transform> Distort, he positions and sizes the new layer containing the traces (**Figure 5.22**), squaring the lines of the traces to the block edges and the streets below. As he did for the buildings, he trims the traces that extend beyond the block surfaces by activating the Pen-tool paths he drew earlier, creating selections and inverting them, and then pressing the Delete key to remove the excess.

His last steps are to adjust the lighting and color of the image, adding stroked paths of red and yellow to simulate headlights and taillights. He uses adjustment layers to heighten the saturation, then hand-paints red and black into selected areas with a layer mask (**Figure 5.23**). Houston as you've never seen it.

Figure 5.22

Figure 5.23

Featured technique
Layer masks

CHAPTER 6

Painting with Images

"My favorite stock images are conceptual ones. What better conceptual icon than a lighthouse? Safety, guidance, warnings of danger—not to mention rough waters!

For me the question became: How can I take it further? A lighthouse as viewed from the sea in the midst of a storm would be a great shot. It's also the kind of image that I love to do: the type that Photoshop makes possible. In light of the fact that I get seasick very easily, Photoshop, in this case, can serve as a very effective lifeboat—not only saving me time and money, but rescuing me from a great deal of discomfort, distress, and even danger."

Client: Stock photograph published by Stone, a division of Getty Images

Lighthouse

To the Lighthouse

As the raw material for this image, Lund used a photo he'd taken a few years earlier at Pigeon Point (about a 40-minute drive south from his studio in San Francisco) of a beautiful 110-foot-high lighthouse. The day was drizzly and overcast—"Perfect, in other words," says Lund. The real lighting would match the storm conditions he planned to create for the image. He'd shot two rolls of Kodak E100S film with his Hasselblad camera that day.

Next stop: Ocean Beach in San Francisco. Near the landmark Cliff House are the ruins of the Sutro Baths—a century-old public swimming facility—which Lund knew provided a good perch from which to zero in on individual waves. Capturing the sea on film at exactly the right moment in time is challenging. Lund avoids that necessity by shooting a series of waves, knowing that he will later composite them into a single scene in Photoshop. This approach affords him the flexibility to overlap, rotate, and darken the waves to achieve his creative vision.

He waited for a blustery, semiovercast day, then shot the waves with his Nikon and an 80-to-200mm zoom lens.

For the final element, he turned to what he calls "the most treacherous terrain yet": his filing cabinets of transparencies. There he found a dramatic cloudy sky shot in Santa Fe, New Mexico, with a Fuji Panorama camera. "I love skies shot with the Fuji panoramic camera," he says, "because with the large-size film, I can choose many different portions of one sky to make up the composite. Often I paste the entire sky into the file and move it around to try various positions until I find the sections I like."

The lighthouse keeper: Lund had taken this shot of Pigeon Point Lighthouse, located on the Northern California coast, for a bank campaign years earlier.

A gathering storm: The sky above Santa Fe was shot on Kodak E100S using a Fuji 617 Panorama camera.

Tossed by the sea: The waves were shot one windy afternoon near the Cliff House at San Francisco's Ocean Beach.

Making Waves

To make the sky look even more ominous, Lund duplicates the sky layer and nudges the duplicate down and to the right. He makes a layer mask of the top layer and paints in the darkest clouds, removing even the slightest glimpse of sunshine.

To create the turbulent ocean, Lund combines several individual wave images. He uses layer masks to paint the waves together into one roiling sea.

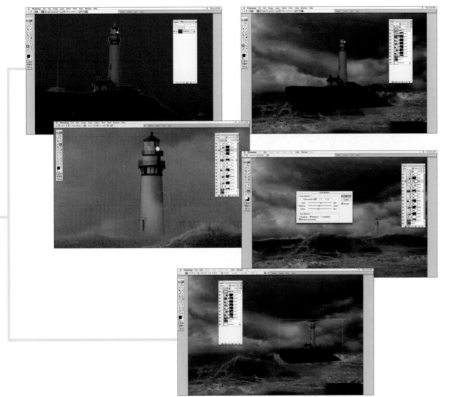

Adding the lighthouse to the image is a straightforward process of outlining it with the Pen tool, converting the resulting path to a selection, and then pasting it into the composite. After scaling it, Lund adds a layer mask to fade the image into the background. He adds dimension by duplicating the layer, darkening it, hiding it with a layer mask, and then painting it back in along the right side. A Color Balance adjustment layer shifts the color toward gray.

To increase the drama of the image, he crops and rotates it slightly so that the waves appear to be bigger and more treacherous from the viewer's perspective.

For the beam of light emanating from the lighthouse, Lund first draws a path where he wants the light to shine. He then converts the path to a selection. He brightens the beam selection by nudging up Curves.

THE LAYERS

How the image stacks up

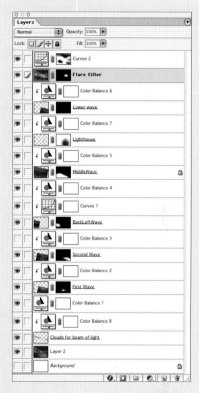

To make it appear as if the beam of light is pointing directly into the viewer's eyes, Lund applies a bright Prime Lens Flare filter to the lighthouse beacon. A layer mask set to Hide All lets him control the size and scope of the flare.

Using Layer Masks to Combine Image Elements

A technique that Lund employs over and over again is using layer masks to do what he thinks of as "painting with images." This allows him to add or delete portions of different images so that they blend together. If you have two image layers stacked on top of each other, you may want to remove some of the top layer so that the bottom layer shows through, giving the effect that the bottom layer is somehow part of the top layer. One way to do this is to apply a layer mask to the top layer, so that when you paint on it with your brush, you gradually add or remove portions of that top layer, revealing the layer below.

The real power of layer masks rests in the way they let you control how much material is removed or added—and where. Layer masks can be very precise—for example, if you want to add a shadow around a doorknob, you can use a small brush to add just a crescent of darkness. Layer masks can also be quite audacious—for example, if you want to blend together storm clouds, you can use a larger brush to merge them into a tempest. Layer masks make it easy to experiment with different effects—and if you don't like what you've done, you can simply remove the layer mask without damaging the image.

Somewhat similar to an alpha channel, layer masks are grayscale channels in which the shades of gray correspond to the opacity or transparency of data in an image. But whereas alpha channels can be used anytime and anywhere, layer masks are specific to a given layer. Layer masks appear in the layer palette as black, white, or gray thumbnails. As with alpha channels, the rule of thumb is that black obscures an area, while white exposes an area. That means when you paint on a layer mask, you paint with black to conceal an area, white to reveal an area, or shades of gray to make areas semitransparent.

When adding a layer mask (Layer> Add Layer Mask) you're given the option to Reveal All or Hide All. Reveal All means that you start with "reveal" as your beginning state (indicated by a white icon in the Layers palette), and painting with black will hide portions of the image. Hide All means that you start with "hide" as your beginning state (indicated by a black icon in the Layers palette), and painting with white will reveal portions of the image.

"I choose whether to Reveal All or Hide All by simply looking at the image and evaluating what I have to do," Lund says. "If what I want to achieve is mostly hiding areas, it makes sense to start with Hide All—there's less painting to do."

The choice of the paintbrush you use is instrumental to the layer mask's effect. Lund most often uses a soft-edged brush (indicated by its fuzzy edges in the Brushes palette), which he sets to Airbrush mode because it can build up or wear away coverage gradually. Varying the size and shape of the brush also alters the effect. Generally, smaller brushes yield more precision, but Lund says they can result in choppy strokes if not used carefully.

"Using layer masks is the most fun part of Photoshop," Lund says. "I get instant results, so I can see how the image is coming together as I work. I can change and experiment and try new directions while I'm making the composite. In short, it really feels like I'm painting with images."

Layer masks can be used in many ways for a variety of situations. The most basic technique—and the one that springs to mind when we think of compositing—is combining elements from individual images into a seamless whole, as Lund does in "Lighthouse."

Step 1: Darkening the sky
As with most of his images, Lund begins the composite with the background—in this case a foreboding sky.

The use of layer masks starts here. He wants to make the sky even more ominous, so he blends two copies of it to emphasize the darkest clouds: He duplicates the sky layer and drags it down and to the right, then adds a layer mask (Layer> Add Layer Mask> Hide All) to the copy (**Figure 6.1**). Setting the foreground color to white (reveal), he paints in the second cloud layer with a soft-edged Airbrush (**Figure 6.2**).

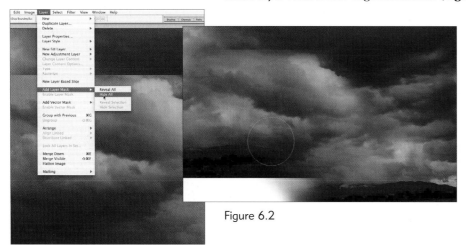

Figure 6.2

Figure 6.1

To blend the layers smoothly, he switches to a smaller brush size and toggles back and forth between painting with white and black, alternately hiding and revealing the second image until it has the look he wants (**Figure 6.3**). (A shortcut for that toggle is to press the X key.) "This is a good starting point, although I may change the clouds later as the image warrants," Lund says.

Figure 6.3

Step 2: Adding wave after wave

With the sky looking suitably threatening, Lund turns to the sea. He opens, copies, and pastes one of the wave images into the main document, and positions it with Edit> Free Transform (**Figure 6.4**). He adds a layer mask (Layer> Add Layer Mask> Hide All), then begins painting the wave into the scene with a fairly small brush (1000 pixels in a 108-MB image). He takes care not to leave any abrupt edges along the side of the new layer (**Figure 6.5**).

He opens and adds another wave to the composite, this time setting the new layer's opacity at 50% so he can better see where he wants to position it (**Figure 6.6**). Once it's in place, he returns the layer to 100% opacity and makes another layer mask (Layer> Add Layer Mask> Hide All). He'll paint that away following the same process as before (**Figure 6.7**). "No rocket science here," he comments. He continues placing and painting in waves with layer masks until he gets the effect he wants (**Figure 6.8**). "As I add more waves I have to start zooming in and using a smaller brush to blend the waves into to each other," he says. Eight layers of waves later, Lund has what he wants—for now (**Figure 6.9**).

Figure 6.4

Figure 6.5

Figure 6.6

Figure 6.7

Figure 6.8

Figure 6.9

Figure 6.10

Step 3: Checking the cropping

"I know I will be cropping the final image, so even though I'm not ready to do a final crop, I check my cropping temporarily just to check things out," he says (**Figure 6.10**). He grabs the Crop tool from the toolbar and crops the image so that the focus will be on the distant lighthouse. Rotating it slightly enhances the sense of peril. Then he executes an Undo. "I'm not ready to make the final decision on that yet," he says.

Step 4: "Painting" the lighthouse

Now Lund adds the lighthouse to the composite. He opens the original image, creates a path around the lighthouse and its hillside with the Pen tool, converts the path into a selection, and copies and pastes the selection into the composite (**Figure 6.11**). After using Free Transform tool to size, rotate, and position the lighthouse, Lund says his first thought is, "This will never work!" But he says, "At some point in almost every image I think that, so I go on." He creates a layer mask (Layer> Add Layer Mask> Hide All), then paints the lighthouse into the image, letting it fade into the waves at the bottom (**Figure 6.12**).

Figure 6.11

Figure 6.12

Step 5: Playing with position

With the lighthouse roughly in the right place, Lund returns to the sea, repositioning and resizing a couple of waves; then he reactivates the masks, and with a fairly small (127-pixel) brush set to medium hardness, fine-tunes them (**Figure 6.13**). "I continue to reposition waves, paste them in, and mask them—in general, make a mess—until the ocean finally starts to look right," he says.

Deciding he wants to reveal more of the sky, he now links the layers containing the waves and the lighthouse (by clicking in the box to the immediate left of the Layer icon), so he can drag them in unison to a new position lower in the frame (**Figure 6.14**).

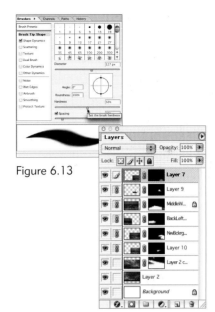

Figure 6.13

Figure 6.14

Step 6: Adjusting color

Now is a good time to coordinate the color. Using adjustment layers (Layer> New Adjustment Layer> Color Balance, checking Group with Previous Layer), he works on the sky and waves. The sky becomes a menacing gray when he removes some of the yellow in the midtones (**Figure 6.15**). He applies similar adjustments to all the individual wave layers, giving the back-left wave an adjustment with Curves (Layer> New Adjustment Layer> Curves) to lighten it in addition to adjusting the Color Balance as before (**Figure 6.16**). Having done that, the sky now looks "a little off," he says, so he returns to the adjustment layer that's already in place. He switches it to Highlights and moves the yellow slider to –15 (**Figure 6.17**).

Figure 6.16

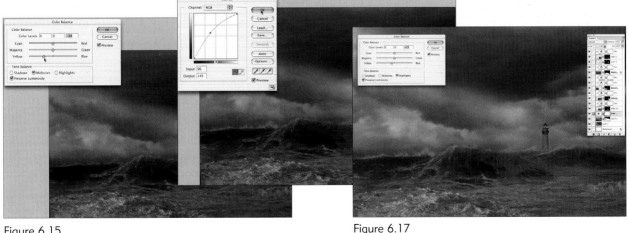

Figure 6.15

Figure 6.17

It's this constant back and forth, evaluating and adjusting, that results in a realistic image. "In the case of the waves, the constantly undulating cloud cover required that each wave have slightly different color adjustments," Lund says. "It's a visual judgment call rather than a quantitative formula. In other words, move the slider till it looks right."

Step 7: Adding dimension

Lund now works on adding dimension to the lighthouse, by duplicating the lighthouse layer and lightening it with Curves. He then activates the layer mask of the new layer and "paints away" the lighthouse along the right edge (**Figure 6.18**). He darkens the lower lighthouse layer with Curves, links the two lighthouse layers, and merges the linked layers (Layers> Merge Linked). He adds a new layer mask to this new layer (Layer> Add Layer Mask> Reveal All), and with a brush set to 1500 pixels and 31% flow, brushes away "just enough of the lighthouse to give the feeling of atmospheric haze," as he puts it (**Figure 6.19**). He also makes the lighthouse railings less blue.

Figure 6.18

Figure 6.19

Step 8: Creating light

A rotating beam of light that pierces the darkness is emblematic of a lighthouse, so Lund creates a flash of light as his last major image element. He links the two sky layers and merges them (Layer> Merge Linked). He outlines the conical path of the intended light beam with the Pen tool (**Figure 6.20**), converts it to a selection with a wide, 33-pixel feather (to give it the soft edges of light being diffused by clouds and fog), and Command/Ctrl-J (layer> New> Layer via cut) turns this selection into a new layer.

Command/Ctrl-M brings up Curves, which he uses to increase the brightness (**Figure 6.21**) and take down the blue. The next touch is to add the bright flare of light that makes the beacon appear to shine into the viewer's eyes. This gets tricky. The Lens Flare effect Lund wants to use must be applied to a single layer. He creates a new layer that holds a flattened copy of the layers he wants to affect by creating a new layer at the top of the stack, and with the new layer selected, holding down Option/Alt and choosing Layer> Merge Visible. Copies of all the visible layers are merged together into the target layer, leaving the original layers intact.

Figure 6.20

Figure 6.21

He opens Filter> Render> Lens Flare and sets the Brightness to 75% and lens type to 105mm Prime (**Figure 6.22**). "How did I arrive at my settings? You guessed it. It took me at least 10 tries to get the amount, type, and positioning figured out," he notes. He changes the position of the lens flare by clicking on the image thumbnail in the dialog box. "And of course, when you click, the effect moves to about a millimeter from where you clicked. So you have to click where you *almost* want it to be," says Lund. He adds a layer mask (Layer> New Layer Mask> Hide All) and paints the flare back in just where he wants it (**Figure 6.23**).

Figure 6.22

Figure 6.23

Step 9: Correcting the light

The final tweaks are tonal corrections. Using two adjustment layers
for Color Balance and Curves, respectively, he adds blue back into the
"beam" layer ("Layer 11 in my poorly named stack," he notes wryly) and
darkens the overall image in a new top layer. Finally, he activates the
mask of the Curves adjustment layer, and with the foreground color set
to black and an 862-pixel soft brush he paints over the darkest clouds
and blackest waves to lighten them a bit (**Figure 6.24**). It's smooth sailing from here on.

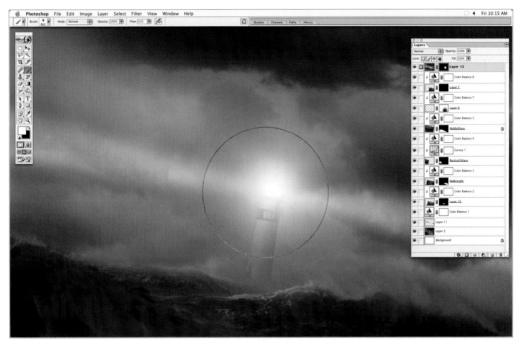

Figure 6.24

Featured techniques
Layer masks
Adjustment layers

CHAPTER 7

Working with Layer Masks

"Ever since I began working with computers, I have had a love-hate relationship with them. At times I even feel, well, dominated by technology. It was this paradox that I set out to describe with 'Dominatrix.'

The first problem: Where to find a model? Should I shoot a real dominatrix? As I discussed this with several folks, at least two of my female friends offered to model. One not only volunteered but also went on to say she had taken dominatrix classes. With several women lobbying to pose for the shot, my wife Dianna suddenly became interested. Not surprisingly, she got the job.

My only disappointment (besides the fact that I could never get Dianna to wear the outfit again) is that the image mostly sells to illustrate pornography on the Internet."

Dominatrix

Cracking the Whip

Lund's first task was finding the outfit. San Francisco offered several options, and he found a leather shop not too far from his studio. "As we talked to the saleswoman about the outfit, we learned a number of things that I don't need to go into here," says Lund cagily. In the end he was happy with the costume but shocked at the price. "It cost me nearly $900—and you can't return that stuff!" he says.

For a location, Lund decided that the concrete floor of his studio would be just fine, but the walls and background would need some work "I wanted a dungeon feel," he says. He looked through his files for a background that would work, settling on an image of a weathered stucco wall he had photographed in Spain.

That decided, it was time for the shoot. Dianna agreed to model as long as her face would not be visible in the image—or in this book. "She was a little embarrassed by the whole thing," Lund says. The plan all along was to replace her head with a monitor so her face would be safe from view, but Lund was careful to not include her head in any of the images that illustrate the steps in this book.

After Lund laced Di up in the corset and boots, he says, he gave her the whip and handcuffs and told her to get into the spirit of the character, then knelt on the floor with a wide-angle lens on his Hasselblad and began to shoot. (He used Kodak E100S film with a 50mm wide-angle lens on the medium-format camera.) "As I directed Dianna through various poses, I continued to suggest that she get into the character," Lund remembers. "'Say 'Crawl, you pathetic loser!' I suggested helpfully. Di only replied, 'Hurry up! I can't breathe and I am about to fall over!' So much for the romance of a photo shoot."

The pain in Spain: A 35mm slide that was shot almost 30 years ago, this is actually the exterior wall of a building in Spain.

Displaced display: The monitor on John's cluttered desk, shot with a Canon D1s digital camera. When Lund went back to find the image for the purposes of this book, he realized he hadn't saved the original—and as it was a digital shot, there was no film to rescan. He recreated the scene here and vowed to "never do that again."

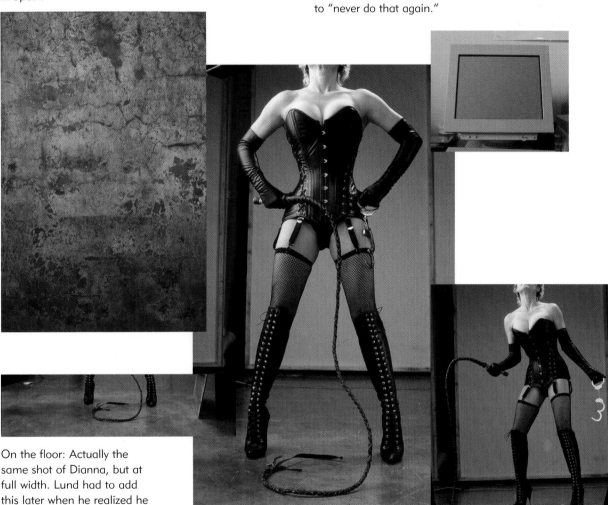

On the floor: Actually the same shot of Dianna, but at full width. Lund had to add this later when he realized he had scanned the first image with too tight a crop.

Role playing: Model (and Lund's wife) Dianna had a difficult time keeping her balance in the stiletto-heeled boots—not to mention breathing in the tight corset—but she cracked the whip convincingly.

Whip it: Dianna gets into the swing of it.

The Ties that Bind

To create the lighting effect on the rear wall, Lund duplicates the wall layer, lightens it up, creates a layer mask, and paints the shafts in and/or out using a large, soft brush. "I wanted to give the impression of a shaft of light from an unseen window," he says. To change the wall from red to olive, he uses a Hue/Saturation adjustment layer.

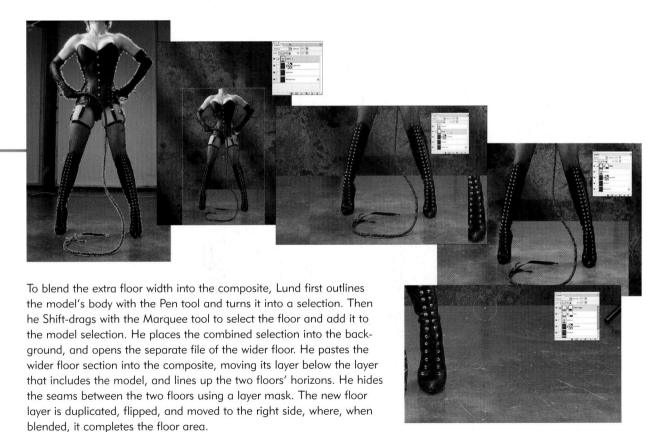

To blend the extra floor width into the composite, Lund first outlines the model's body with the Pen tool and turns it into a selection. Then he Shift-drags with the Marquee tool to select the floor and add it to the model selection. He places the combined selection into the background, and opens the separate file of the wider floor. He pastes the wider floor section into the composite, moving its layer below the layer that includes the model, and lines up the two floors' horizons. He hides the seams between the two floors using a layer mask. The new floor layer is duplicated, flipped, and moved to the right side, where, when blended, it completes the floor area.

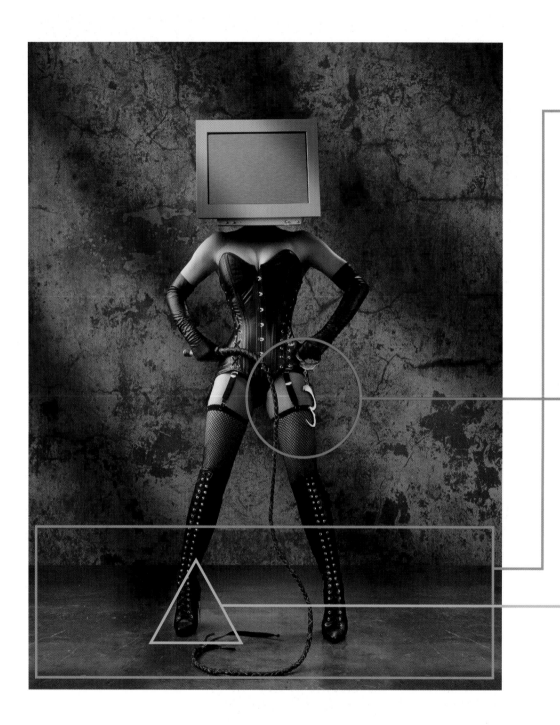

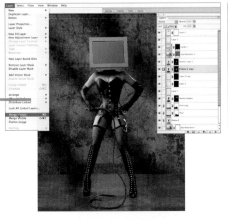

To polish the floor, Lund links the layer holding the model and floor with the two floor layers and merges them into one layer. He sets the Burn tool to Midtones, and with a large, soft brush blends the line along the back of the floor. Then he uses the Healing brush to mend the scar of a vertical reflection on the right side.

Lund decides the handcuffs—an essential part of any dominatrix ensemble—need to stand out more, so he selects them with the Pen tool and creates a new layer. He can now paint a very light gray into the contours of the selection to give the handcuffs a reflected sheen. "I make a new layer so if I screw up it's not a big deal," he says.

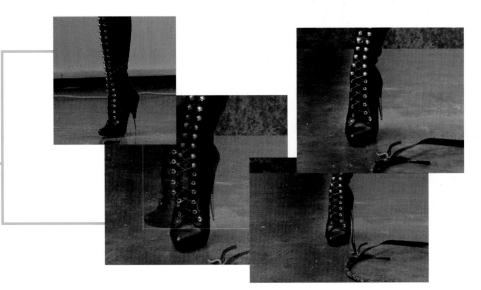

The spike heel on Dianna's right foot isn't visible, so Lund opens the other Dianna image and, zooming in, outlines the shoe with the Pen tool. He turns the path into a selection and pastes the heel into the Dominatrix composite. He creates a layer mask, then paints in the new heel. To create the heel's reflection on the polished floor, he duplicates the heel layer and flips it vertically, then paints it into the floor with a layer mask.

When Lund shot the monitor, he ignored what was on its screen. To blank out the monitor he selects the screen area with a Polygonal Lasso tool; next he applies the Add Noise filter set to Gaussian (which adds a grainy texture, to make the screen look like it's full of static) and then the Motion Blur filter (which simulates side-to-side movement, to add turbulence to the static onscreen).

After placing the monitor on the model's neck, Lund decides that he doesn't like the keystone effect—the angle of looking up at the monitor ("even though I shot it that way thinking it would add impact," he says). So he uses the Transform tool's Distort function to straighten out the monitor's edges and make it smaller.

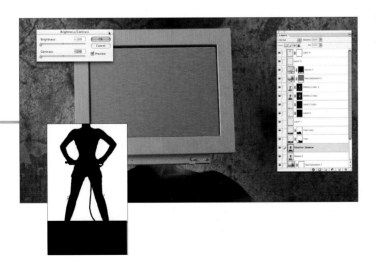

To create the shadow cast by the monitor on the dominatrix, Lund first duplicates the layer that includes Dianna, then decreases the contrast and brightness by moving both sliders to the far left. The figure on this new layer now appears as a black figure against a white background. He'll use this layer to create the shadow. He next creates a layer mask (Layer> Add Layer Mask> Hide All) for this shadow figure and paints in the shadow around her neck with a soft brush. "Since the shadow layer is a duplicate of the Dianna layer, when I paint the shadow in, it will never go beyond the boundaries of the model's body in the Dianna 2 layer," he says. "Clever, eh?"

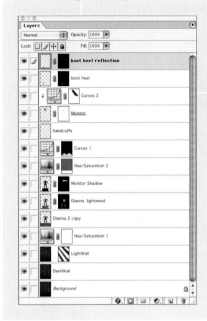

THE LAYERS
How the image stacks up

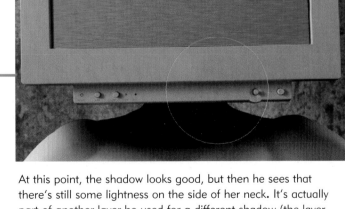

At this point, the shadow looks good, but then he sees that there's still some lightness on the side of her neck. It's actually part of another layer he used for a different shadow (the layer named "Dianna 2 copy"). He switches to that layer, activates the mask on that layer, and paints away the offending portion.

Enhancing Images with Layer Masks

In the previous chapter, we saw Lund's technique for painting with images to blend them together. We also provided glimpses of other ways in which layer masks can be used—to add special effects, for example. The beauty of layer masks is that they can be used in so many ways.

"Layer masks are wonderfully versatile," Lund says. "Once you master the basic technique of painting layers in and out, you'll find you use them for just about anything. You have complete control over the appearance and amount of image, light, or effect shown, so you can do as much or as little as you like with them."

In "Dominatrix," Lund uses layer masks to blend two floors together, apply a special effect to a wall, and add highlights and shadows to the central figure and her costume. He also employs several adjustment layers.

Adjustment layers can affect all the layers beneath them, or be limited to just the layer beneath it. They can also, using the built-in layer mask, be applied to specific areas of the image. The general image controls (Image> Adjustments) do not have the flexibility of the built-in layer masking.

"I'm kind of quirky and inconsistent about how I adjust color," Lund concedes. "But in situations where I need to be precise in my color tinkering, I prefer to use adjustment layers because the color possibilities are endless and I can always go back and make further adjustments later on—which I almost always do."

Step 1: Creating shadows and light
The first layer mask Lund uses is on the background. He's going to add a lighting effect that makes it seem as if sunlight is streaming in from an unseen window.

After opening the wall file and duplicating the background layer, he sets the duplicate layer's blend mode to Multiply and its opacity to 30% (**Figure 7.1**), and names the layer DarkWall. He duplicates the original background layer yet again, names it LightWall, moves it to the top of the layer stack, and sets its blend mode to Screen.

"I use the Multiply blend mode to darken and the Screen blend mode to lighten," Lund says. Blend modes apply color transformations based on color data. The colors in the top layer interact with those in the layer below to produce a specific effect. Photoshop's Layers palette includes 22 such blend modes, but Lund uses only a handful of them. "By using a layer mode, I can fine-tune the layer instead of having to apply the effect to the entire image—as I would have if I had used brightness or some other effect. I didn't use an adjustment layer (this time, anyway) because it was easier to apply Multiply to the entire layer."

Figure 7.1

Lund now adds a new layer mask to the LightWall layer (Layer> Add Layer Mask> Hide All) (**Figure 7.2**). He then selects a large soft brush of 1399 pixels (in an 82-MB image)—"That's just the number I got when I moved the slider"—selects white as the foreground color (remember that white reveals) and paints several diagonal strokes across the image (**Figure 7.3**). Shift-clicking when dragging the brush ensures that the lines will be straight. The layer mask icon in the Layers palette shows (with white lines) where Lund has painted on the mask, exposing the LightWall.

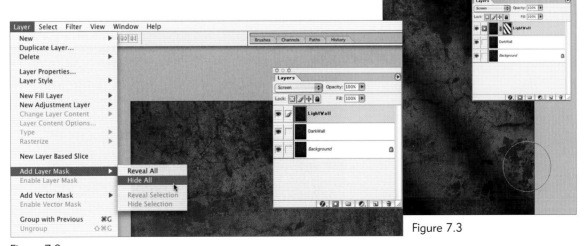

Figure 7.2

Figure 7.3

Step 2: Constructing the image

Now he starts building the scene, layer by layer. First he draws a path around the model with the Pen tool (**Figure 7.4**). He converts the path to a selection with a 1-pixel feather (Paths palette menu> Make Selection). He adds the floor to that selection by Shift-dragging with the rectangular Marquee (with a slightly softer 2-pixel feather) across the floor just under the power cable in the background. He copies, then pastes this combined selection into the wall background, sizing and positioning the figure with Edit> Free Transform (**Figure 7.5**). He names this layer Dianna 2.

Figure 7.4

Figure 7.5

Step 3: Merging the floor panels

Lund uses the next layer mask to construct a seamless floor from two images to cover the width of the composition. This step came about because of a blunder: Lund cropped the image containing the figure too tightly, but didn't realize it until after he had already Pen-tooled the model and done other work. Thinking on his feet, he decided that it would be easier to use a layer mask to blend a second, wider floor into the first than to rescan and start all over. "Even though I'm pretty fast with the Pen tool, it wasn't worth tracing her again," Lund says. "This is another instance when layer masks saved the day."

He opens the file that contains the uncropped floor, selects all (Command /Ctrl-A), then copies it and pastes it into the composite. In the Layers palette, he moves this new floor layer below the Dianna 2 layer (**Figure 7.6**) to check that the horizons align before moving it back to the to the top of the layer stack. He creates a layer mask (Layer> Add Layer Mask> Reveal All), setting it to Reveal All because there's more of this floor to reveal than conceal (**Figure 7.7**). With a 494-pixel soft brush, he paints away the new floor on the right and center, blending the new floor with that on the Dianna 2 layer (**Figure 7.8**). Floors, like skies, are rarely uniform, so blending the two lets Lund control how the gradations of light on the floors—shown at two magnifications, no less—match up.

Figure 7.6

Figure 7.7

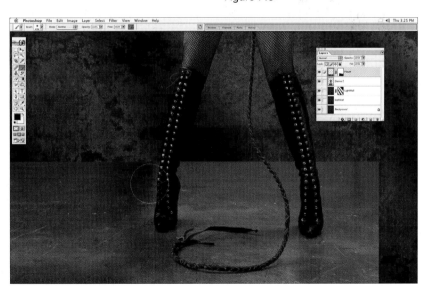

Figure 7.8

After duplicating the floor layer, he flips it (Edit> Transform> Flip Horizontal) to create a symmetrical floor and eliminate the errant, over-size boot left over from magnifying the uncropped floor. After positioning the flipped floor layer to align it with the other floor, he touches up the joined floor layers using a 267-pixel brush.

Step 4: Adjusting the directional lighting

With the image assembled, Lund is ready for the fine-tuning: adding highlights and shadows to the model and her gear.

Lund duplicates the Dianna 2 layer and moves it to the top of the layer stack. He goes to Image> Adjustments> Brightness/Contrast and moves the Brightness slider to –41 and the Contrast slider to –27 (**Figure 7.9**). Like many of Lund's Photoshop techniques, he uses his photographer's eye to watch and evaluate color adjustments on the fly (keeping the Preview box checked helps, too).

After adding a Layer mask (Layer> Add Layer Mask> Hide All), he uses a 422-pixel soft-edge brush, and with the foreground color set to white, paints up the inside of her right thigh and down the outside of her left thigh (**Figure 7.10**). This applies a shadow that mirrors the directional light of the background. He gives the same treatment to her arms and neck (**Figure 7.11**).

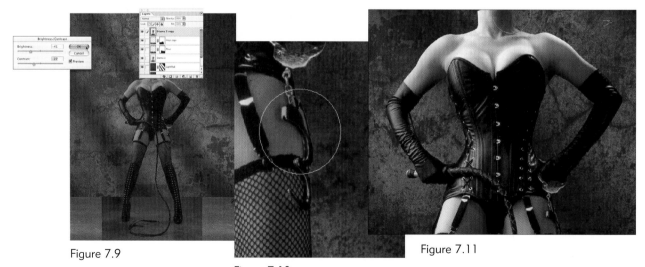

Figure 7.9

Figure 7.10

Figure 7.11

Step 5: Adding highlights to leather

Lund duplicates the Dianna 2 layer again, this time to adjust the lighting on the leather costume. He drags the new layer to the top of the stack and sets the layer's mode to Screen. "If I know I have to brighten with Screen or darken with Multiply, I duplicate the layer first before setting the mode. Then it's easy to play with the opacity slider to fine-tune the results," Lund says.

Screen lightens the image dramatically (**Figure 7.12**). He creates another layer mask (Layer> Add Layer Mask> Hide All) and with a 166-pixel brush paints highlights into the leather (**Figure 7.13**). When he's finished, he thinks the highlights look too bright, so he reduces the layer opacity to 50%.

Figure 7.13

Figure 7.12

Step 6: Fine-tuning the shadows

Taking a critical look at the image, Lund notices a dark patch to the left of the model's left boot. When put in the context of the wall shadows, it just doesn't look right to him. He decides he needs to readjust the shafts of light on the back wall so that the shadow hits the floor just where the dark patch is.

To make that change, he goes to the Layers palette and clicks the link symbol between the LightWall image icon and its layer mask icon to decouple the two (**Figure 7.14**). Using the Move tool, he drags the mask to the left until the shadow falls over the dark area on the floor. (Holding the Shift key constrains the movement to one direction.) The layer mask icon in the Layers palette reflects this change (**Figure 7.15**). With a soft, 1399-pixel brush, Lund retouches the background using the layer mask, continuing the stroke of light now cut off by the mask's edge (**Figure 7.16**) and adding another shaft of light in the upper-right corner.

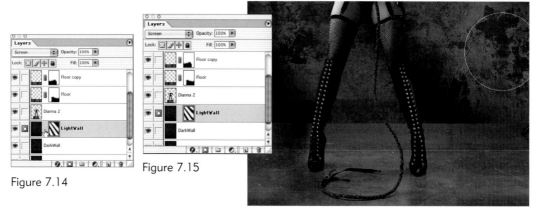

Figure 7.14

Figure 7.15

Figure 7.16

Step 7: Using adjustment layers to adjust color casts

Using blend modes like Screen and Multiply are all well and good, but Lund wants to apply some specific color adjustments, which means using adjustment layers. From time to time Lund uses all three general methods of making color adjustments—image adjustments, layer modes, and adjustment layers—but he prefers adjustment layers, as they give him both precision and flexibility.

Adjustment layers offer the same effects as the general image adjustments like Levels, Curves, and Color Balance, but Lund explains the difference like this: "If you like to live dangerously, work directly in the file, which is what you do when you apply image adjustments. You alter the pixel information of the file, and each time you do, each time you go back and make another change, you degrade the quality of the image," he says. "With adjustment layers I get more flexibility in my adjustments—I can change the dynamics of a curve in a specific area rather than simply lighten or brighten a layer, and I can also go back and readjust the image without compounding the image degradation."

Lund clicks the LightWall layer and goes to Layer> New Adjustment Layer> Hue/Saturation (**Figure 7.17**). He moves the Hue slider to +42 and the Saturation slider to –27, leaving the Lightness slider at 0 (**Figure 7.18**). The wall color becomes less pink. Again, Lund's technique is guided more by intuition than training. His analysis of his color-adjustment technique is simple: "I do what looks right."

Next he alters the color of the floor. "I zoom in until the floor is as big as I can get it and still see it side-to-side," says Lund. "Is that a light stand on the right? I'll fix that later." He uses the rectangular marquee, set with a 2-pixel feather, to select the floor. Command/Ctrl-H hides the "marching ants" of the selection so that he can see the junction between the wall and the floor more clearly. He then goes to Layer> New Adjustment Layer> Hue/Saturation, and moves the Hue slider to +14 and the Saturation slider to –11, leaving the Lightness slider at 0 (**Figure 7.19**). The result brings the floor color into harmony with the wall color.

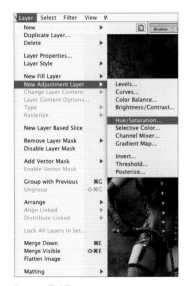

Figure 7.17

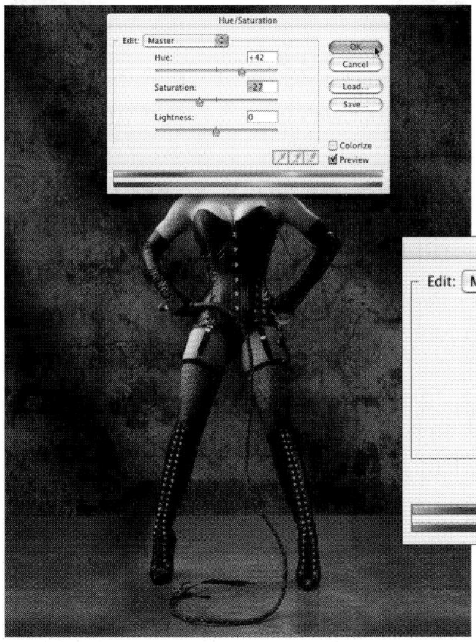

Figure 7.18

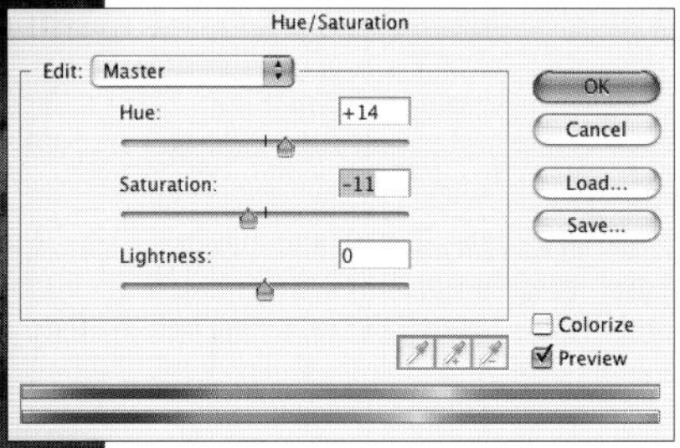

Figure 7.19

"The floor color now is consistent with the wall color...but the Dominatrix now looks a little too magenta," he notes. "See, too, that the layer icon for the adjustment layer, in the Layers palette, is black above the line of the floor, which means that the adjustment layer is not affecting anything in the black area" (**Figure 7.20**). He activates the layer mask by clicking on its icon, then inverts the marqueed-floor selection (Select> Inverse). Now, the floor is no longer selected, but everything else is.

With the layer mask activated, he picks a medium gray for the foreground color, holds down the Option/Alt key, and presses Delete. This deletes the black area of the mask and makes it the gray of the foreground color. Remember that if black conceals and white reveals, gray is halfway in between—semitransparent. Thus we have a semitransparent mask in our adjustment layer that affects everything but the floor. This semitransparent mask is what shifts her coloring toward green, but only mildly (**Figure 7.21**). The floor has a white layer mask over it.

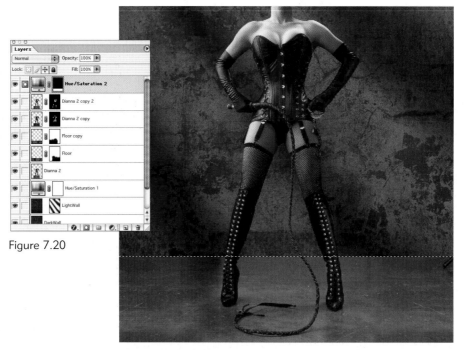

Figure 7.20

Figure 7.21

Lund makes further color corrections until everything is to his liking. He darkens the floor with a Curves adjustment layer, checking the Group with Previous Layer option in the Curves dialog box. Then, with the Curves layer mask active, he uses a black paintbrush in the layer mask to lightly brush the floor, the boots, and the whip to remove some of the darkness he just created.

Step 8: Adding new objects with layer masks

A layer mask can also be used to paint in something that didn't exist before in that position. The spiked boot heel doesn't show in the head-on shot of the model, so Lund lifts the boot from the other photo using the Pen tool (**Figure 7.22**). "Although only the heel will be seen, I want the whole boot in case I need to show more when I make its reflection," he says. "Showing the boot heel is a nice detail." Lund adds: "Besides, I paid $250 for those boots—I want to see that heel!"

Figure 7.22

He pastes the boot into the composite, changing its opacity to 64% to better position it against the background and resizing it with Free Transform (**Figure 7.23**). (He ups the opacity again after he places the layer.) With a layer mask (Layer> Add Layer Mask> Hide All) and the foreground color set to white, he paints in the portion of the heel that's needed (**Figure 7.24**).

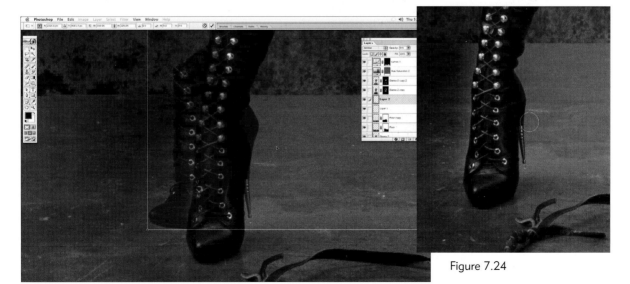

Figure 7.24

Figure 7.23

Then he creates the heel's reflection in the polished floor. He duplicates the heel layer and flips it (Edit> Transform> Flip Vertical). After activating the layer mask, he uses a 277-pixel brush at 0% hardness (as soft as he can possibly make it) and paints with black to fade away the heel reflection to a more realistic appearance (**Figure 7.25**).

Figure 7.25

Step 9: Adding the monitor's shadow

Lund is now ready to add the monitor head to the image. He uses the Pen tool to create a path around the monitor, which he converts into a selection; he then copies, pastes, sizes, and positions it into the composite. Not liking the monitor's angle, he squares it with Transform> Distort. Then, with the Polygonal Lasso tool, he selects and deletes the rounded portion of the monitor base just above the model's neck. He duplicates the Dianna layer, names the new layer Monitor Shadow, and takes its brightness and contrast down to zero (**Figure 7.26**). He creates a layer mask (Layer> Add Layer Mask> Hide All) and paints in the shadow under the monitor with a 504-pixel soft brush. When he sees some residual lightness left over from an earlier shadow layer (Dianna 2 copy), he locates that layer mask, activates it, and paints out the offending lightness. A few final adjustments of light on the monitor, and he's done. Mercy!

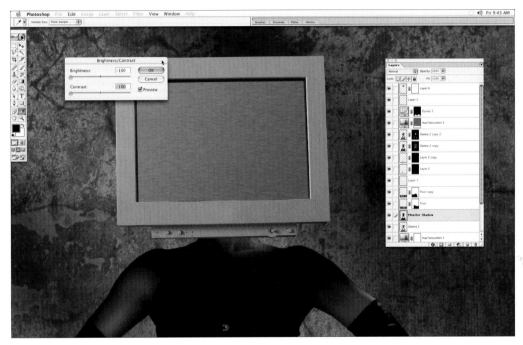

Figure 7.26

PART III

Using Filters

One of Adobe Photoshop's most notable features is its filter technology. Filters allow you to add all kinds of special effects to images. For example, the Pointillize filter converts an image into a pattern of dots, like the pointillist effect made famous by Impressionist painter Georges Seurat. Other filters are less artistic but more practical in nature. The Unsharp Mask filter (Filter> Sharpen> Unsharp Mask), for example, lets you selectively enhance detail in an image. There are hundreds of filters available from Adobe and from third-party software developers. Some filters—like De-Interlace Video—are highly specialized, while others—Plastic Wrap, for example—have limited usefulness and border on just plain goofy.

The easy, eye-catching effects made possible by Photoshop filters tend to unleash the artist within Photoshop jockeys. Photoshop purists often scoff at those who would take a mediocre image, apply a filter effect to it, and call it "art." In the hands of a Photoshop master, however, filters can be used to great advantage.

Lund chooses his filters wisely, drawing primarily on less splashy but technically important filters such as Gaussian Blur (Filter> Blur> Gaussian Blur), which blurs the edges of pixels for smoother transitions. But there are a few visual-effect filters that he finds useful, as well: Liquify, Radial Blur, and Spherize, as well as Lens Flare, which we saw in action in "Lighthouse" (Chapter 6).

The Liquify filter's distortions can make impossible images seem real. Here, Lund shows what it can do to a face (in this case, his).

Introduced somewhat recently, in Photoshop 6, the Liquify filter (Filter> Liquify) is essentially a Photoshop brush that lets you smear, push, or otherwise distort parts of an image. The effect is similar to pulling taffy. You can choose from a variety of distortion modes, such as Pucker or Bloat, vary brush size (and therefore the area to be affected), increase brush pressure (the degree of distortion), and specify which areas of the image should remain untouched, among many other features.

Liquify's effect could be viewed as a cheap gimmick, but as you'll see in this section, Lund uses it for surprising and outrageous effects—such as transforming a fingernail into a devilish claw. "Liquify gives me god-like powers and solves an amazing and unexpected variety of problems," he says.

Another of Lund's favorite filters is Radial Blur—or more specifically, Radial Blur with the Zoom option turned on. This filter can add a sense of speed and dimension to an image. Lund says, "Radial Zoom Blur is not a filter I use often, but it solves a problem that is otherwise almost unsolvable—indicating forward motion of something that is moving straight at you, whether it's a locomotive or an explosion."

The Radial Blur filter with Zoom (which Lund calls Radial Zoom Blur) is an effective tool for creating the effect of fast forward

On occasion Lund will turn to Spherize (Filter> Distort> Spherize), which produces the effect of looking into a convex fun-house mirror. "Many filters, while not useful in everyday imaging, are essential to specific imaging challenges," Lund notes.

In this section, you'll see how Lund uses each of these effects in several different ways—and how a little filter finesse can go a long way.

The Spherize filter can make flat objects seem three-dimensional. This wrecking ball started out as a manhole cover.

Featured technique
Liquify filter

CHAPTER 8

Reshaping Natural Elements

"In coming up with stock photography ideas, I always try and make it a practice to look at the opposite of whatever idea I am working on. It was natural, then, that having just completed an angel image for a magazine assignment my thoughts turned to the idea of doing an image of a devil. And from years of looking into the mirror each morning, I knew that I would make a very good devil.

The image sells well—about a dozen times a year! A friend let me know that he had seen it used in the *National Enquirer* to illustrate a story on the Pope selling souls to the Devil."

Client: Stock photograph published by Getty Images

The Devil

To Hell and Back

Lund began by having his assistant photograph him in black-and-white mode with a Leaf DCB (Digital Camera Back) mounted on a Hasselblad camera. One of the earliest digital cameras for studio photographers, the DCB captures color data in three exposures—one each for red, green, and blue, with each one taking about a minute. Not convinced he could sit still for that long, he opted for a single-pass black-and-white exposure, to which he later added color in Photoshop. Looking into the camera, he beckoned with his index finger: "I wanted not just an image of a devil, but of temptation itself," says Lund.

While Lund is the first to admit that his hair is, shall we say, "thinning," he looked elsewhere for the perfect bald head on which to affix the devil's horns. He shot the more rounded dome of his friend Mary Liz, who had lost her hair as a result of chemotherapy (she's just fine now, thanks).

He crinkled up *seamless*—a paper material that comes on large rolls commonly used by pro photographers as backdrop—and lit it from underneath to give the background a cave-like, underground quality. For the horns, he photographed a pair of deer antlers. "I could shoot the background and antlers in color because, unlike me, they wouldn't fidget during a three-minute exposure," he explains. For the final touch he found a shot of flames in his stock files.

The background: Crinkled seamless can look like hell.

Horns of a dilemma: John's wife Dianna found these deer antlers on a walk.

More found horns.

The Devil himself: "Finally, an image that suits me."

Bald is beautiful: John's close friend (and head model) Mary Liz beat cancer.

"Follow me": Leading you into temptation.

The flames of purgatory: Aim a jet of spray paint at a candle and look for fireworks.

Fan the fire: Flop the flames for symmetry.

The Devil's in the Details

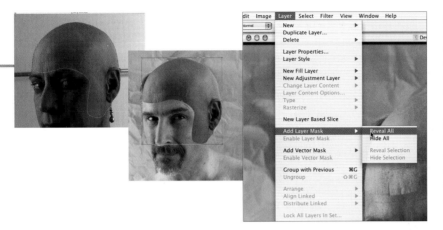

Mary Liz's scalp covers up what little hair John has left. Lund selects the desired area with the Pen tool, then copies and pastes over his head. To merge the bald pate more seamlessly with his own, Lund uses the Pen tool's Paths setting to select the reshaped head and torso, then eliminates the tuft of hair on the left and brings the skull curve inside of the tip of the ear. (He can leave the tuft on the right, which he will cut around when he selects the head later.) After color correcting with Curves, he uses a layer mask to paint away the hard edges with a soft brush.

Lund cuts and pastes the antlers into place. Then, to form the ridge of flesh, he uses the Burn and Dodge tools to create highlights and shadows. He runs the Burn tool in an arc around the base of the horn, using a series of short strokes to create a shadow, then positions a second shadow arc about a brush width away from the first. For the highlight, he brushes down the length of the arc in between the two shadows with the Dodge tool.

To cast the horn's shadow, Lund makes a new layer, then selects the darkest color on the horn. With a soft airbrush, he paints that color in short strokes from the center of the horn's base towards the Devil's eye. He uses the Smudge tool to fine-tune the shadow's shape. Finally, he sets the shadow's layer opacity to 62 percent.

Lund selects the distorted head and hand with the Pen tool, copies and pastes them into the background, then colorizes them with the Hue/Saturation controls.

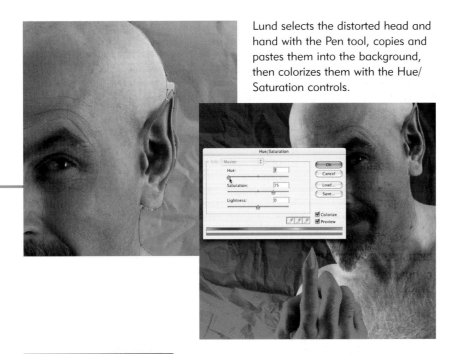

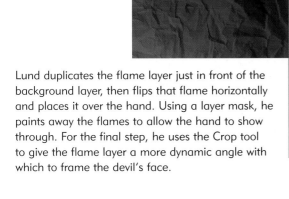

Lund duplicates the flame layer just in front of the background layer, then flips that flame horizontally and places it over the hand. Using a layer mask, he paints away the flames to allow the hand to show through. For the final step, he uses the Crop tool to give the flame layer a more dynamic angle with which to frame the devil's face.

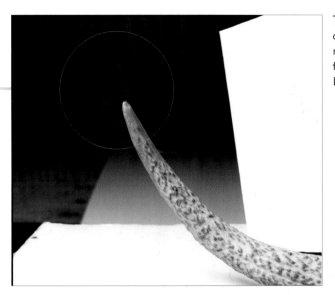

The antler is distorted into a more devil-like form using the Liquify brush.

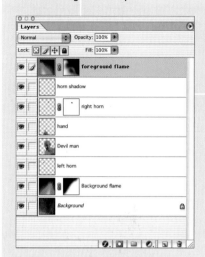

The Liquify brush does a superb job on fingernails!

Using the Liquify Brush to Reshape Reality

The Liquify brush (Filter> Liquify) is a quick and efficient means of distorting an image. "The Devil," with its elongated visage, spiky horns, gnarled claws, and pointy goatee, shows some of its more useful effects. This filter, which opens in its own window, has many variables to it—distortion modes (Turbulence or Twirl, for example), tool options (Brush Pressure and Jitter), and the ability to "freeze" areas to protect them from change—but Lund mostly uses the Liquify brush's default Warp tool, which pushes and pulls the image pixels to give the effect of dragging a finger through thick batter. He adjusts the brush size and pressure according to the amount of distortion desired and the size of the area he's working on.

Step 1: Elongating the face

Lund begins his devilish transformation by narrowing the face. To lend his physiognomy a more fiendish appearance, he uses the Liquify brush's Warp setting (Filter> Liquify> Warp Tool) to elongate the head. The Warp tool can produce subtle or dramatic transformations, depending on the length and force of the mouse drag, so Lund finds it gives him the best control over his distortion. A couple of swipes along the jaw with a brush size large enough to cover the beard (300 pixels) and a brush pressure of 50 do the trick. He then sharpens the beard to a point using a smaller brush of 121 pixels (**Figure 8.1**).

Figure 8.1

Step 2: Sharpening the ear

Using an 85-pixel setting, Lund uses Liquify again to stretch the ear into batlike peaks (**Figure 8.2**). The same brush settings are used to arch the devil's eyebrow (**Figure 8.3**). Lund notes that the appropriate brush size will vary according to your tastes. Larger brushes produce pronounced effects quickly but with less precision. Smaller brushes give you more control.

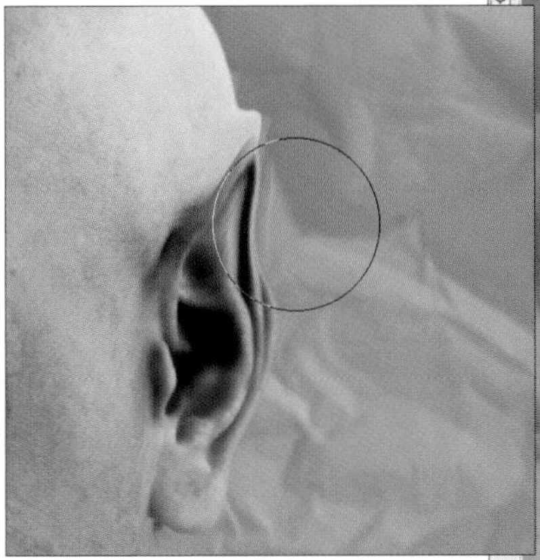

Figure 8.2

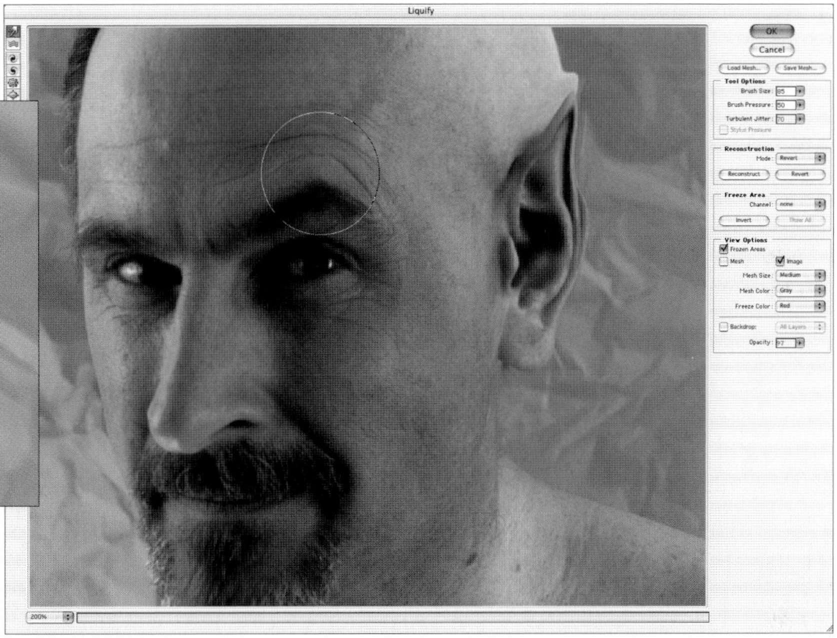

Figure 8.3

Step 3: Adding a glint

To give the eye a mischievous glint, Lund drops the brush size to 1 pixel for better precision as he distorts the pupil into a diamond-like shape (**Figure 8.4**). With all Liquify brushwork, Lund advises reducing brush pressure if the brush becomes hard to control.

Figure 8.4

Step 4: Sharpening his claws

Claws are essential to any self-respecting devil. Opening the image of his beckoning hand, Lund reshapes the fingers between the knuckles to create a gnarled look. He tapers the nail to a menacing tip with a few strokes of a 79-pixel brush (**Figure 8.5**). Again, Lund recommends experimenting to get just the right effect. Next he uses the Pen tool's Path setting, as before, to select the modified hand, makes it into a selection, and copies and pastes the hand into main image, creating a new layer above the figure. He then positions and sizes the hand with the Free Transform tool (**Figure 8.6**).

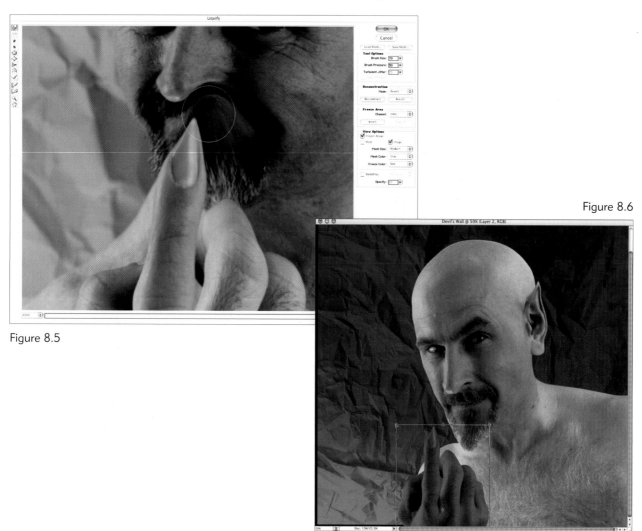

Figure 8.6

Figure 8.5

Step 5: Adding horns

The devil is now ready for his horns. Lund opens the first image of deer antlers (**Figure 8.7**) and makes the horn stubbier by pushing down on its tip with the Liquify brush's Warp tool (**Figure 8.8**). He sets the brush at 358 pixels with a Brush Pressure setting of 50. He applies short strokes with the same brush size and pressure settings to contort the shortened tip into just the right curve (**Figure 8.9**).

Figure 8.8

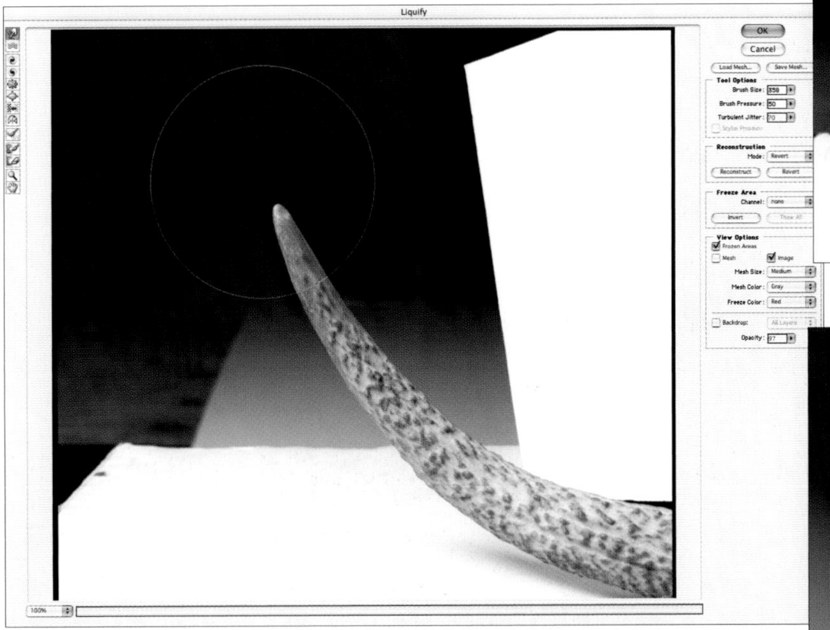

Figure 8.7

Figure 8.9

Lund then uses the Pen tool to select the part of the horn he wants to use (**Figure 8.10**). He creates a selection, and copies and pastes it into the main image as a new layer. He positions it so that it will appear to emerge from behind his head and resizes it using Free Transform. He then places this layer underneath the one containing the Devil (**Figure 8.11**).

Figure 8.11

Figure 8.10

Step 6: Rounding the horn

He repeats the process with the second horn, positioning it on the right of the devil's head. Adding a layer mask, he paints with the air-brush around the base of the horn to achieve the proper roundness (**Figure 8.12**).

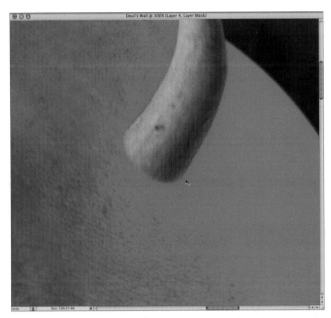

Figure 8.12

Featured techniques
Liquify filter
Shadows
Highlights

CHAPTER 9

Creating Dimensional Distortion

"To create an image to illustrate biotechnology, I felt a good starting point would be a model with a shaved head. Shaved heads are often viewed as futuristic and even robotic. If I composited various high-tech gadgets onto the model's face, I'd accomplish my objective.

Finding the right technological pieces for the different parts of the head wasn't easy. Replacing one of the model's eyes with a lens seems a too-obvious choice—although obvious choices can sometimes be good ones. On the other hand, I spent several days puzzling over how to treat the mouth. I tried putting a speaker into the lips, but it just wasn't working.

About this time I paid a visit to my son Chasen. He had on his latest pair of high-tech-looking, outrageously expensive sunglasses. It dawned on me that the frame portion of his glasses would, if properly altered, make a great mouthpiece."

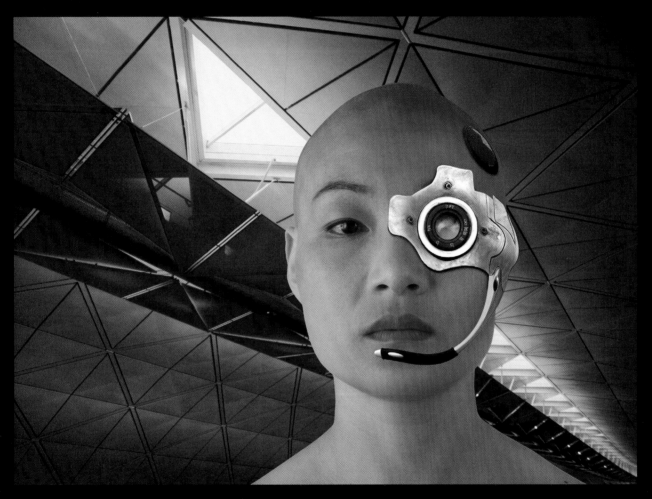

Client: Stock photograph, unpublished

Tech Woman

Tomorrowland

The background, shot at an airport in Asia ("Tokyo, perhaps? I've forgotten," Lund says) is from Lund's files. (The fact that he can't remember the exact location adds to his personal sense of technological dislocation when he views the composite, Lund says.) The airport image looks as if it's been manipulated with Photoshop's Hue/Saturation controls, but this is the way Lund shot it. "I had photographed the scene with color infrared film without the recommended yellow filter, so the result was a monochromatic purple image, very geometric and futuristic looking," he explains.

The model, however, he does remember: It's Barbara, a professional model who has produced memorable work with a number of San Francisco photographers. Her shaved head gives her an androgynous look.

The lens for Tech Woman's eye came from an old Polaroid camera that no longer worked. Lund took the camera apart and photographed many of its pieces: the lens, the metal housing, various wires, and other details.

The ear posed a problem. "I wanted to show a device that suggested how hearing might be affected by technology, but the position of the face didn't show enough of, or a good angle of, the ear," says Lund. He selected the Polaroid's focusing mechanism, which reminded him of a speaker or microphone, then distorted it for the correct angle and perspective and pasted it onto the model's forehead.

Lund shot the sunglasses in the backyard. "I had my son put his glasses down on a step in the open shade of his house and grabbed a couple of shots with my 35mm camera," Lund explains. "Back at the studio, I scanned them in, and voilá."

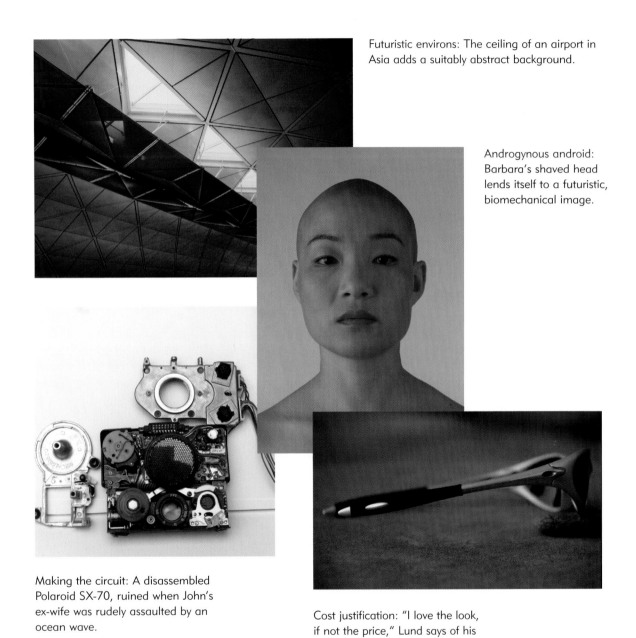

Futuristic environs: The ceiling of an airport in Asia adds a suitably abstract background.

Androgynous android: Barbara's shaved head lends itself to a futuristic, biomechanical image.

Making the circuit: A disassembled Polaroid SX-70, ruined when John's ex-wife was rudely assaulted by an ocean wave.

Cost justification: "I love the look, if not the price," Lund says of his son's sunglasses.

One Step Beyond

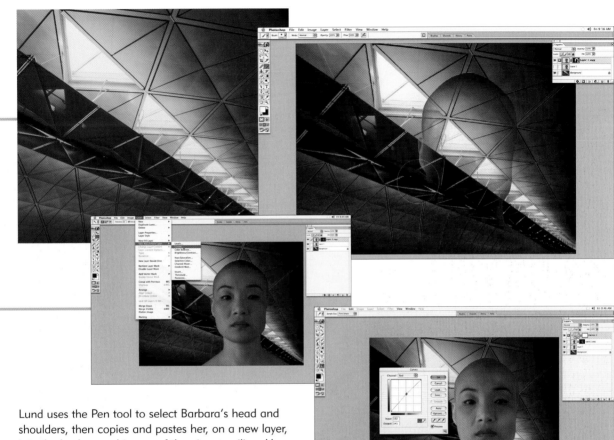

Lund uses the Pen tool to select Barbara's head and shoulders, then copies and pastes her, on a new layer, into the background image of the airport ceiling. He duplicates this new layer, then adjusts its color balance so she looks more natural in her new environment. After making a layer mask, he uses a large, soft airbrush to paint the perimeter of her head and shoulders. The result is a slight color cast on the edges of her body that would appear if she were actually in this environment. When working on the layer mask, Lund turns off the original Barbara layer so he can see what he's doing. Softening the edges with the Blur tool avoids a cut-out look.

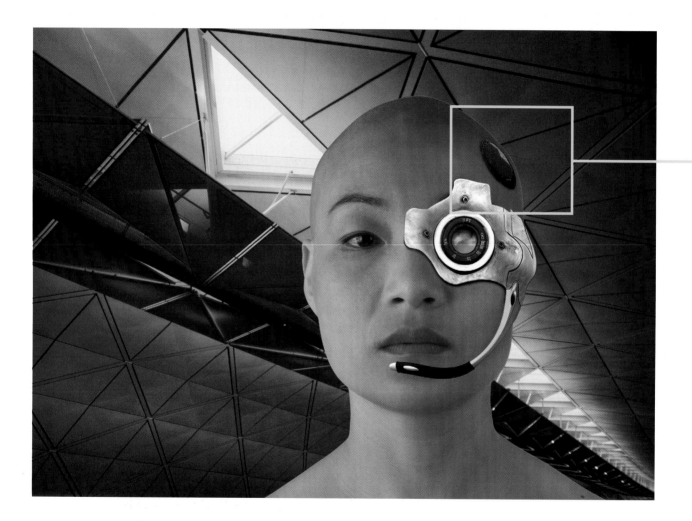

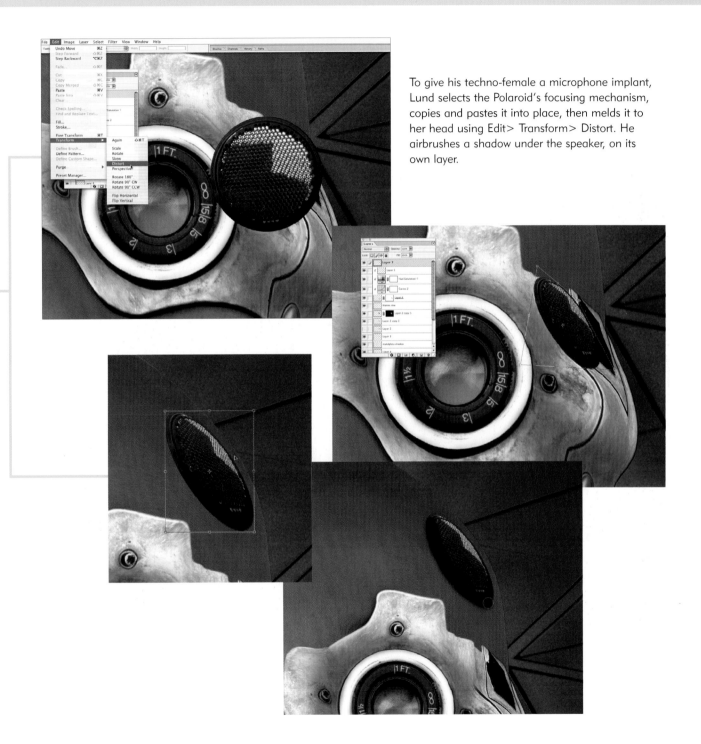

To give his techno-female a microphone implant, Lund selects the Polaroid's focusing mechanism, copies and pastes it into place, then melds it to her head using Edit> Transform> Distort. He airbrushes a shadow under the speaker, on its own layer.

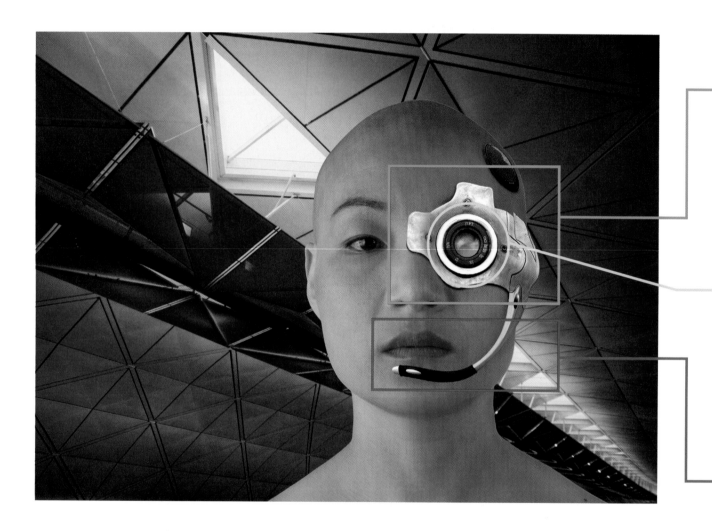

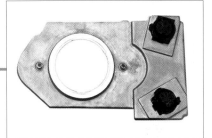

After selecting, copying, and pasting the metal plate over Barbara, Lund uses the Liquify brush to warp the metal so that it follows the contours of Barbara's face. He duplicates, then darkens, the copy of the metal-plate layer. Then, using a layer mask, he paints the appropriate shadows from the darkened layer onto the light metal plate.

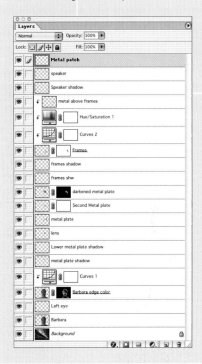

To make a futuristic eye, Lund selects the lens of the Polaroid SX-70 and pastes it into place behind the metal plate, also a relic of the destroyed camera. When creating the selection, he is careful to draw the path just inside the edge of the metal. That way, when the selection is made with a 1-pixel feather applied, no traces of the background will show.

He places the sunglasses frame in the image and shapes it into a mouthpiece using the Liquify filter.

Adding Dimension with Liquify, Shadows, and Highlights

In "The Devil," Lund used the Liquify filter to make natural elements—the human body and deer antlers—look supernatural. Now, in "Tech Woman," Lund goes to the opposite extreme, creating a futuristic scene of an androgynous figure in a plastic, high-tech environment. He digs deeper into the Liquify brush here—using its Freeze and Reconstruct tools when warping the metal headset and curving the mouthpiece. He also employs layer masks to create shadows and textures to give the distorted objects dimension. As a result, these unreal elements look superrealistic, at least in the context of the image.

Step 1: Adding the eye plate

Using the Pen tool, Lund selects the upper metal plate, making sure to cut out the center hole, from the image of Polaroid camera parts (**Figure 9.1**). He then uses the Clone Stamp tool to clean any up any imperfections or unwanted details. Free Transform is used to size and position the pasted-in metal plate (**Figure 9.2**).

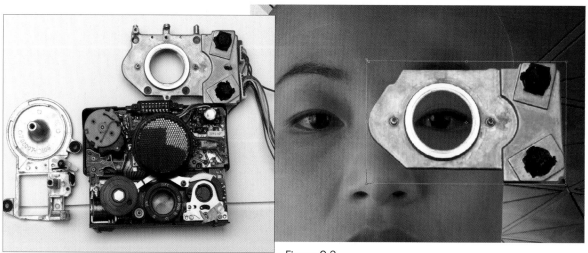

Figure 9.1

Figure 9.2

Step 2: Forming it to the head

Next, Lund duplicates the metal plate layer and turns it off—he likes to keep one in reserve. With the original layer active, he opens the Liquify filter (Filter> Liquify) and checks the Backdrop option so he can see the shape of the head through the transparent background ("actually I tend to go back and forth between seeing the background and not," Lund says). Before he begins using the Warp tool, Lund clicks on the Freeze tool from the Liquify toolbar (**Figure 9.3**) and paints over the eyehole to protect it from distortion (the frozen areas are indicated by red) (**Figure 9.4**). With the Warp tool, he then uses a series of small strokes to push the metal plate from the right edge in, so that it follows the contours of the face (**Figure 9.5**).

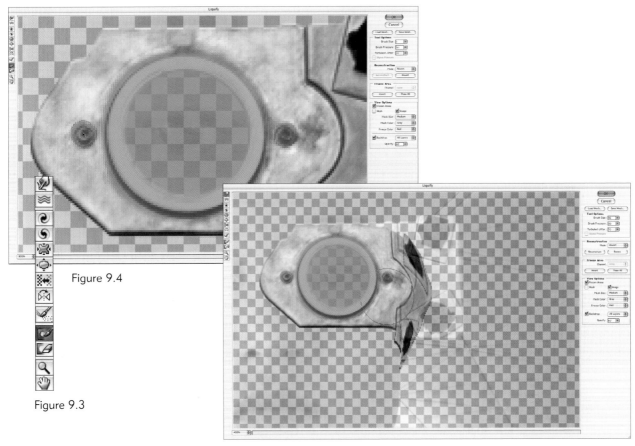

Figure 9.4

Figure 9.3

Figure 9.5

Step 3: Backing up

Distortion can go too far, of course. The Liquify filter includes the Reconstruct tool (located just above the Freeze tool), which lets him restore the distorted area to its original state (**Figure 9.6**). For detail work, such as working on the left-hand bolt, Lund zooms way in, uses a small brush, and works with the Backdrop setting turned off (which he says is less distracting) (**Figure 9.7**). With this, as with most of his work in Photoshop, Lund does a lot of experimenting before he gets it the way he wants it.

Figure 9.6

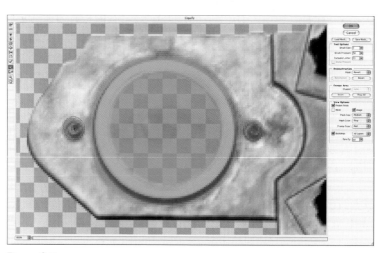

Figure 9.7

Step 4: Trying again

Even after this step, the artist in Lund isn't satisfied. He's pleased with everything except the top part of the plate near the eye, where the dark eyebrow shows (**Figure 9.8**). This is where that duplicate layer comes in. He makes it visible by clicking the Eye icon in the Layers palette, duplicates it (to create another spare), and then uses the Liquify brush to reshape the left-hand edge of the metal plate. "After a lot of trial-and-error that I won't bore you with, I end up rotating the second metal plate 90 degrees clockwise and adding some shaping," he says (**Figure 9.9**).

Although he likes the new effect, most of this second plate isn't needed. So using a layer mask, Lund paints away the lower portions of the new metal plate, leaving just the tab on top.

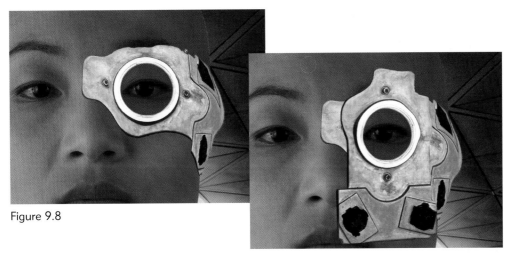

Figure 9.8

Figure 9.9

Step 5: Adding highlights

Now it's time to add dimension to the headset—faces aren't flat, so neither should the headset be. First, to give the metal some sheen as if light is bouncing off curved surfaces, Lund brushes the Dodge tool (Brush: 12 pixels, Exposure: 16 percent) along the top edge of the rotated plate, with Range set to Highlights (**Figure 9.10**). He links the two metal plates by activating one plate in the Layers palette, then clicking on the column to the left of the other plate's thumbnail, and then merging the two (Layer> Merge Linked) (**Figure 9.11**). By merging the two layers he simplifies the highlighting process by painting on just one layer instead of two.

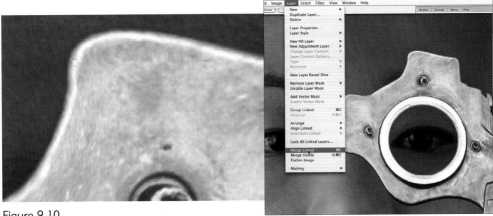

Figure 9.10

Figure 9.11

Step 6: Creating shadows

Had the metal actually had the contours of the model's face, you would see shadows, so Lund adds shading to the headset using layer masks. He duplicates the new merged metal-plate layer and darkens it (Image> Adustments> Brightness/Contrast) (**Figure 9.12**). Then he adds a layer mask (Layer> Add Layer Mask> Hide All) and paints in the areas that should be darker, such as the indented areas of the eye socket and the side of the nose (**Figure 9.13**). He adds some shadow by making a new layer and placing it under the metal-plate layer, then airbrushing the new layer (Brush: 110, Flow: 100 percent, Mode: Normal). If the shadow seems too heavy, he plays with the layer opacity (**Figure 9.14**).

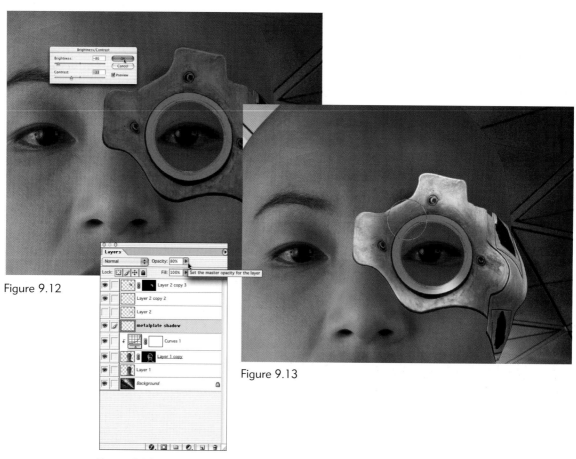

Figure 9.12

Figure 9.13

Figure 9.14

Step 7: Creating a robotic eye

The headset isn't finished yet. For a true robotic look, Lund turns the eye into a camera lens. Returning to the image of his ruined Polaroid camera, Lund uses the Elliptical Marquee tool to select the lens. By holding down Option/Alt-Shift, he drags out a perfectly symmetrical selection from the center of the lens (**Figure 9.15**). He then copies and pastes the lens into the main image and uses Free Transform (Edit> Free Transform) to resize the lens to fit the hole on the plate (**Figure 9.16**).

Figure 9.15

Step 8: Turning sunglasses into a mouthpiece

The mouthpiece completes the headset. He opens the image containing the sunglass frame, selects the frame using the Pen tool, pastes the selection onto a new layer in the main image, and positions it so that it attaches to the side of the metal plate (**Figure 9.17**). Opening the Liquify filter and using the Warp tool with a very large brush, he bends the frame into a curve, using the Background option to better shape it to the face (**Figure 9.18**). Two strokes and it's done. Lund keeps his strokes to a minimum: The fewer strokes, the less bumpy the result, he says.

Figure 9.16

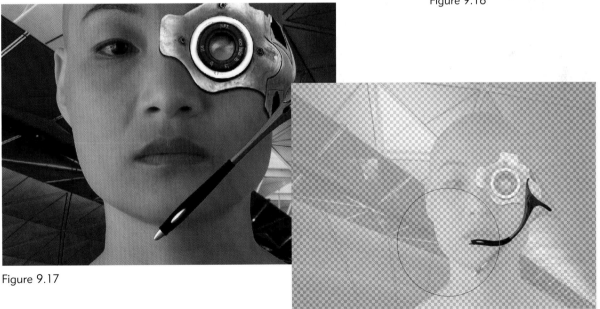

Figure 9.17

Figure 9.18

Zooming in and using a smaller brush, he fine-tunes the distortion. In both cases, he uses a relatively low brush pressure of 22 (**Figure 9.19**). He then uses layer masks to paint away unwanted portions of the frame and the Liquify brush and Free Transform to adjust its angle and position.

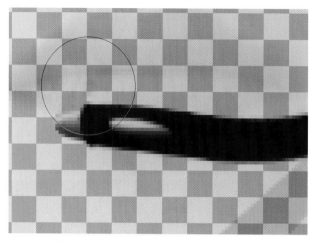

Figure 9.19

Step 9: Adjusting color

The color of the mouthpiece needs to better match that of the headset, so Lund uses layer masks and soft brushes to blend it into the metal below. Then he uses an Adjustment layer (Layer> New Adjustment Layer> Curves), checks the option to Group with Previous Layer, and manipulates the curves to make the mouthpiece's color and lightness better match that of the underlying metal (**Figure 9.20**). Lund finds that adjusting curves alone doesn't do the trick, so he adds another Adjustment layer (Layer> New Adjustment Layer> Hue/Saturation) to reduce the saturation (**Figure 9.21**).

Still not satisfied with the color match, Lund takes radical action. He draws a path with the Pen tool around the area he wants to blend in, makes a selection from the path with a 3-pixel feather, then uses the Clone Stamp tool to replicate the metal color and texture. With Mode set to Color, Aligned unchecked, and Use All Layers selected, he Option/Alt-clicks the area he wants to sample, and with a large brush, paints with the cloned color within the selected area (**Figure 9.22**).

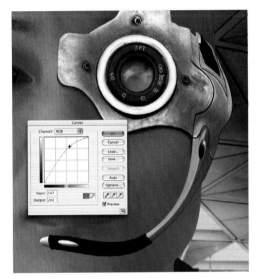

Figure 9.20

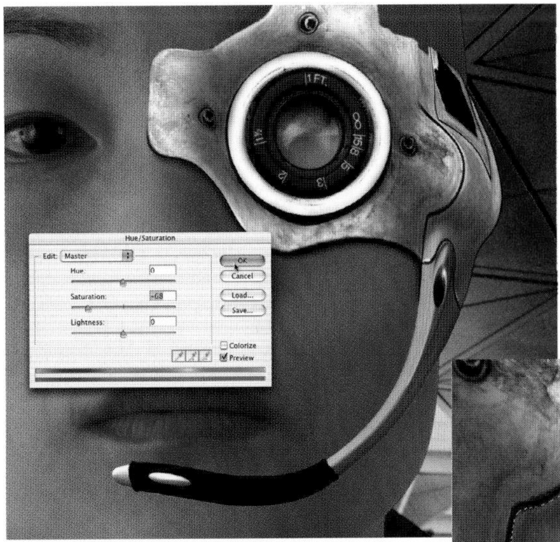

Figure 9.21

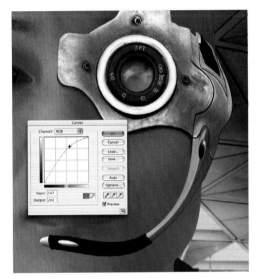

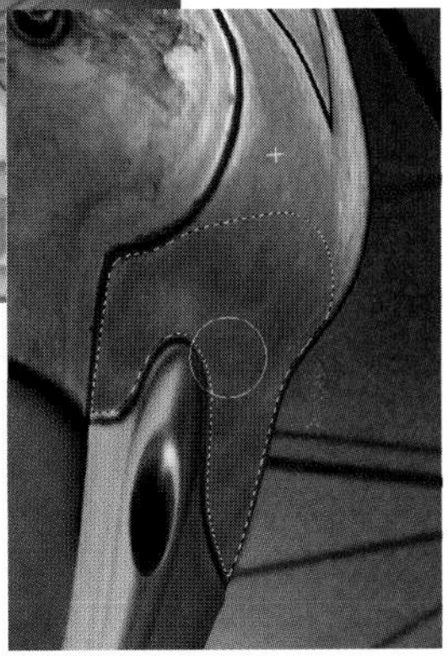

Figure 9.22

Step 10: Repeating the process

Lund uses variations on this method to attach a speaker to the top of the head (using Edit> Transform> Distort), to add shadows beneath the mouthpiece frame and around the speaker (using Layers), and to soften the mouthpiece edges (using the Blur tool). Far out.

Featured technique
Radial Blur with Zoom

CHAPTER 10

Showing Forward Motion

"I wanted to make an image that would illustrate the dangers of being uninformed. I thought an image like that could be used by stock photo clients to persuade their prospective customers to use their goods and services to survive and prosper. My original idea was to show a series of people standing on a hillside wearing blinders.

One day while reading an issue of *Wired* magazine, I saw an ad that featured a close up of a dandelion. In the background, coming directly toward the dandelion, is a jet fighter. The obvious implication was that the dandelion wasn't long for this world. The image had a lot of impact, and I began to think about how I could achieve an image with that kind of drama. Suddenly it hit me: Instead of using an airplane, I could have a train heading towards a blindered businessman.

I reasoned that using a stereotype of English propriety would underscore the message of being rigid and out of touch, and at the same time make it more timeless—less prone to becoming outdated. Using an old steam locomotive rather than a modern train engine added a further iconic quality, as did giving it a sepia color scheme.

This image continues to be one of my best sellers in part, I think, because art directors feel good about themselves when they make the connection between the derby hat and the French painter Magritte."

Gathering Steam

In Lund's mind, the problematical part of creating the image would
finding the locomotive. He wanted to shoot one but couldn't find a
steam engines locally. He checked with some historical photo archi
but no one had a head-on shot of the kind of train he wanted.

The answer: going to a hobby store and checking out the model tra
He found one, barely two inches high that had a good amount of d
Before forking over $200, he checked with the salesperson, who sa
could return it for a small restocking fee.

The next step was to line up a model, rent a derby hat, and begin sho
ing the components. He fashioned the makeshift blinders out of his a
tant's belt and his own wallet. Lund shot the images in black and whi
with a Leaf DCB on a Hasselblad camera.

When the model's scheduled booking was over. Lund stepped in as
back-up model. He always shoots more than he needs, and in this c
he thought he might need additional photos of the hat, the belt, an
the blinders. "I was just goofing around," he says. "But I made sure
use flat lighting in all these shots so that if I had to use any parts f
them, they would match the model shots."

Images of billowing smoke came from Lund's archive—"grab shots"
factories in rural California that Lund snapped on his travels. What'
grab shot? "An unplanned, spontaneous photo," Lund explains.

Shortly after Lund finished the image, while showing the model loc
tive to a friend, he dropped it. "As it turned out, the $200 I spend o
the locomotive was the single biggest expense of the shoot," he say

Self-portrait: Lund wears blinders fashioned out of his assistant's belt and his own wallet—Lund refers to these back-up shots as "spare parts" because you never know when you might need them.

I say, old chap: Model Bill Austin's stiff upper lip.

Inside the beltway: Lund always shoots items individually as well as set within a composition. In this case, he wanted a clear shot of just the belt, just in case he needed all, or part of it, later—and he did.

Burning down the fields: Dense smoke rises as farmers burn off the stubble after harvesting wheat fields in the San Joaquin delta near Tracy. Another photo from Lund's files.

Holy smokes: A grab shot from Lund's files of smoke billowing from refinery stacks along California's Interstate 5.

All steamed up: A Lund file photo of steam escaping from a sugar beet factory in Tracy, California.

Jumping the tracks: Lund found this HO locomotive in a hobby store (the most popular size model train, HO refers to its scale, in this case 1:87).

Full Steam Ahead

After pasting the locomotive image into a blank canvas, Lund sizes and positions it with Free Transform. He then duplicates it onto a new layer, to which he applies the Radial Blur filter with the Zoom option turned on, repeating the process as necessary. Using layer masks, he erases portions of the zoomed areas to give the impression of a locomotive speeding towards the viewer.

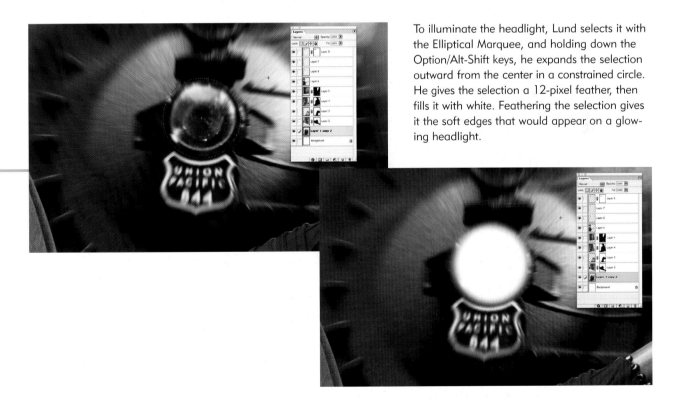

To illuminate the headlight, Lund selects it with the Elliptical Marquee, and holding down the Option/Alt-Shift keys, he expands the selection outward from the center in a constrained circle. He gives the selection a 12-pixel feather, then fills it with white. Feathering the selection gives it the soft edges that would appear on a glowing headlight.

The smoke and steam layers are progressively pasted into and positioned within the main image. With each, Lund adds a layer mask, then paints the best parts into the main image using a variety of soft brushes—from 600 to 2000 pixels—to erase and paint the image on the layer masks. When he's done, the extraneous background is removed and the smoke and steam appear to billow from the engine.

The selected figure, sporting a bumbershoot and derby, is placed into the image in front of the locomotive.

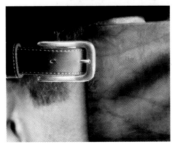

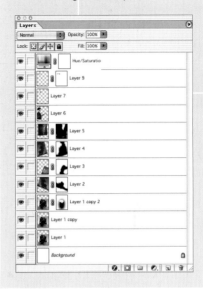

THE LAYERS
How the image stacks up

In comparing the look of the blinders on the model to their look on his backup shots, he decides he likes the lighting on the backup shot better. In that image, he selects the blinders using the Pen tool and converts the paths to selections with a 1-pixel feather. After copying and pasting the blinders into the image of the costumed model, Lund sizes, rotates, and positions them with Free Transform. The Burn and Dodge tools give the appropriate shadows and texture.

To imbue the image with an old-fashioned aura, Lund gives it a sepia tone by creating an Adjustment layer and using Hue/Saturation to alter its color with the Colorize option.

Creating the Illusion of Speed with Radial Zoom

Photoshop's Blur filter has many options, each of which affect an image differently. They can be used for a wide spectrum of uses, from subtly softening a too-sharp image to dramatically changing focus and altering perspective. Motion Blur, for example, creates the illusion of speed as if the object were passing across your field of vision. But what if you want to make an object look as if it's coming straight at you? In "Blinders," Lund uses the Radial Blur filter in its Zoom mode—what Lund calls Radial Zoom Blur—to make a tiny toy locomotive appear as if it's bearing down on an oblivious businessman.

"Applying the filter several times in varying degrees to subsequent layers gives me the flexibility to add just the right amount of effect to the right areas," Lund says. This approach also prevents the effect from looking too abrupt and adds depth to the image.

Step 1: Finding the focus

After creating a new canvas, placing the locomotive image into it, and using Free Transform to give it an appropriate position and size, Lund opens the Radial Blur filter (Filter> Blur> Radial Blur) to bring up a dialog box (**Figures 10.1** and **10.2**). Clicking the Zoom button and the Good button, he sets the Amount to 10—a number he determines through trial and error—and drags the Blur Center in the Radial Blur dialog box over the approximate location of the locomotive's headlight. This will keep the center of the headlight in focus, with the blur radiating outward. Because the amount is set fairly low here, the initial blur is subtle (**Figure 10.3**). It may take a few tries to get it right, so Lund always starts with a small amount of blur as he attempts to find the best location. Lund prefers the Good setting over Best. "The best setting doesn't look natural to me, it's too pristine and artificial," he says. "Good is good and Best is not."

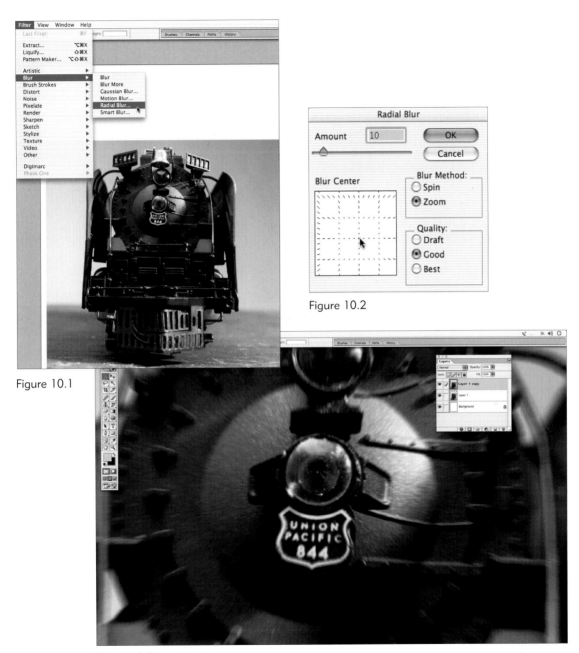

Figure 10.1

Figure 10.2

Figure 10.3

Step 2: Adding change layer by layer

Lund duplicates the blurred layer and opens the Radial Blur dialog box again, moving the Amount slider to 20 but leaving the other settings the same (**Figures 10.4** and **10.5**).

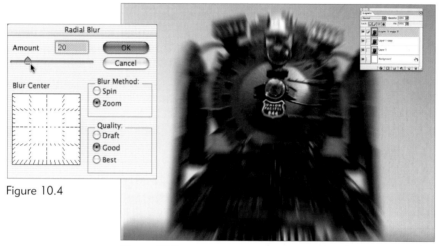

Figure 10.4

Figure 10.5

By building the blur layer by layer, Lund is able to enhance details he likes and obscure those he doesn't. He explains: "The central portion of the train—the headlight, sign, and cow-catcher—has detail I'd like to preserve, but I don't really have a good background. To compensate, I cover the background with smoke, steam, and Blur." Adding new layers with progressively larger amounts of blur keeps the focus on the leading part of the engine but obscures its edges. Lund notes that had he shot a real train barreling down the tracks right at him, the effect would have been similar—the edges are further away from you and therefore less distinct.

Step 3: Blending the layers

To complete the blur effect, Lund blends together the original locomotive and the two blurred layers using a layer mask (Layer> Add Layer Mask> Reveal All) and Photoshop's largest brush (2500-pixels) (**Figure 10.6**).

Setting the foreground color to black, he paints in the layer mask over the headlight—this hides the blurred image where the toy train looks less realistic and keeps the central area in focus.

Figure 10.6

Step 4: Speeding up, slowing down

Lund switches the foreground color to white as he paints on the layer mask to reveal parts of the most-blurred image. By toggling between painting white (reveal image) and painting black (conceal image) he progressively works on the blur at the train's edges to enhance the illusion of speed (**Figure 10.7**). Lund sums it up: "It's very much a visually intuitive process: add speed, slow it down." All in Photoshop, of course.

Figure 10.7

CHAPTER 11

Adding Depth to Flat Objects

"Out with the old, in with the new! That was the concept behind 'Impact!' But perhaps more importantly, this composition illustrates that an 'imagined' image can be more powerful than one shot from life.

When I first decided to make this image, I went to a demolition site in San Francisco and shot a few photos. It was, however, immediately apparent that reality didn't match my mental picture. When I pictured a wrecking ball, I envisioned an iron ball on the end of a chain slamming into a building. By today's demolition standards, it is a tear-shaped concrete device on the end of a cable dropping onto, not crashing into, a building. What I saw in my mind's eye was more graphic and powerful than the actual scene. So I decided to forgo reality and *stay* in my mind's eye."

Impact

Starting from Scraps

As Lund walked back from the demolition site to his studio, ponder how to create the image, it occurred to him that a manhole cover m do as a wrecking ball. It has the right shape, albeit flat instead of ro and its mottled metal surface matched that in his mental picture. I had his Nikon cameras with him, so he stopped on the way to pho graph a manhole cover worn smooth by traffic about a block from studio. While he was at it, he shot images of the sidewalk, includin portion that was cracked.

He finished his image-gathering back at the studio, shooting an ol rusty chain that had been collecting dust for some time, then scroun up a brick and shot several angles of that. His files yielded the rest the images, including a brick wall and pictures of a simulated comp explosion—from "Crash Test Dummy" (see "Adding Impact with Co in Part IV), as a matter of fact. Setting this scene of destruction aga a serene blue sky adds to its power.

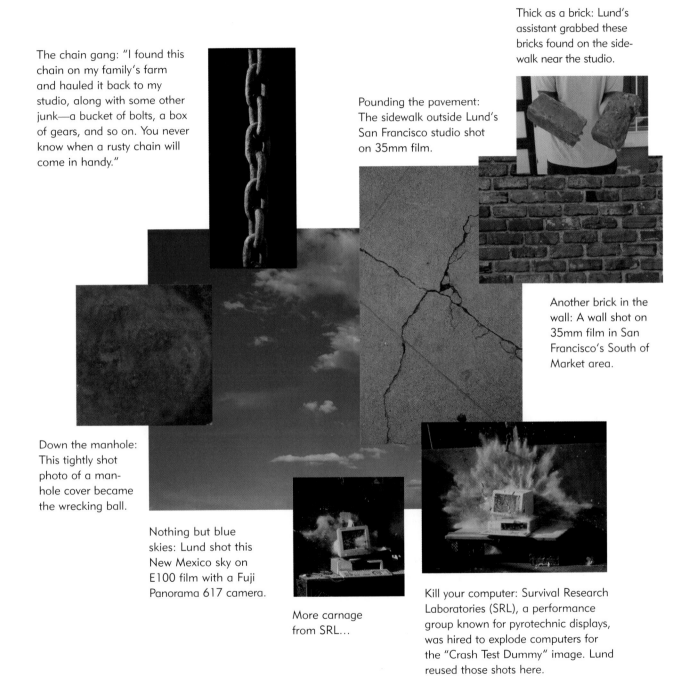

The chain gang: "I found this chain on my family's farm and hauled it back to my studio, along with some other junk—a bucket of bolts, a box of gears, and so on. You never know when a rusty chain will come in handy."

Thick as a brick: Lund's assistant grabbed these bricks found on the sidewalk near the studio.

Pounding the pavement: The sidewalk outside Lund's San Francisco studio shot on 35mm film.

Another brick in the wall: A wall shot on 35mm film in San Francisco's South of Market area.

Down the manhole: This tightly shot photo of a manhole cover became the wrecking ball.

Nothing but blue skies: Lund shot this New Mexico sky on E100 film with a Fuji Panorama 617 camera.

More carnage from SRL…

Kill your computer: Survival Research Laboratories (SRL), a performance group known for pyrotechnic displays, was hired to explode computers for the "Crash Test Dummy" image. Lund reused those shots here.

Like a Ton of Bricks

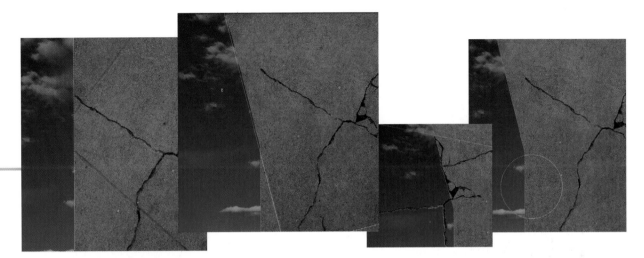

A photograph of cracked pavement becomes the wall of a building. Lund pastes the sidewalk into the image of the clouds and sky. He then duplicates the layer and, because the crack is at the wrong angle, removes the crack from the new layer with the Clone tool.

Back on the original sidewalk layer, he selects the crack using the Magnetic Lasso tool, copies it, and pastes it onto the wall in the desired position. To create the feeling that the wall is toppling, he duplicates the wall layer with the new cracks and uses Transform to position it at an angle. With a layer mask, he paints away the bottom of the new layer with a large (1557-pixel) brush. Now he cleans up the crack itself; he removes the moss using the Hue/Saturation control to fade out its green color.

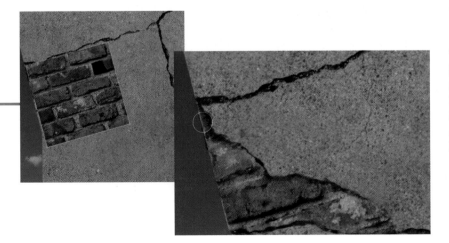

To make it look as if the wrecking ball has knocked off the building's skin to reveal its brick skeleton, Lund pastes in a portion of the brick wall then transforms it for size and position. Adding a layer mask, he paints in the desired bricks.

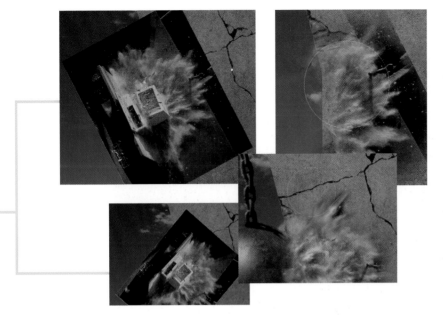

To create the explosion at the point of impact, Lund relies on an old image of a computer being demolished, which he positions and resizes with the Free Transform tool. A layer mask hides the computer, and the dust and debris are painted back in with a variety of brush sizes. He repeats the process with a second rotated image. He'll add one more explosion later on when he decides that the image needs more *oomph*. Applying Radial Zoom Blur to the exploding debris makes the image more dynamic.

At the point of impact, Lund imagines individual bricks hurtling outward, so he opens the image of loose bricks and selects each one with the Pen tool, and pastes them in the image one at a time, using a layer mask to fade the bricks into the explosion.

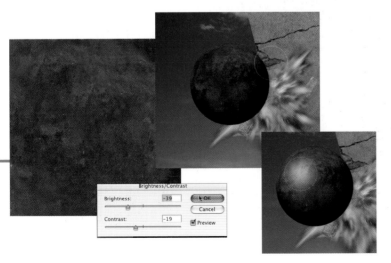

Lund makes a circular selection from the manhole cover, then applies the Spherize filter to it to add depth. He pastes the spherical selection into the image as a new layer. Then Lund duplicates the manhole layer, darkens the new layer, and uses a layer mask to paint the dark layer back in around the lower perimeter of the lighter ball, increasing the 3D effect. Activating the lower wrecking ball layer, he uses the Dodge tool to create a highlight, which adds more depth.

THE LAYERS

How the image stacks up

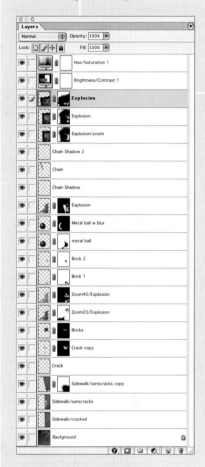

After selecting the chain with the Pen tool and converting the path to a selection with a 1-pixel feather, Lund places the chain in the main image, rotating and sizing as necessary to make it appear as if attached to the ball. He then duplicates the chain layer and adds a Motion Blur filter to it. With the blurred chain layer active, Lund selects the Move tool and taps the left-arrow key to nudge the chain to the left in one-pixel increments until it is offset by 9 or 10 pixels. He paints a shadow for the chain with the Airbrush tool on a new layer, using the Eraser and Smudge tools to refine and reshape it. The Liquify brush adds more curvature.

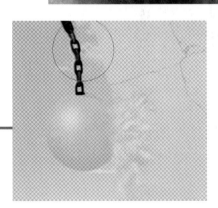

Adding Depth with the Spherize Filter

Photoshop offers many ways of adding the illusion of dimension to flat objects. With 3D Transform, you can create 3D objects by mapping flat images to cubes, spheres, and cylinders. The result is impressive but artificial-looking. Lund prefers a more natural effect. In "Impact!" he transforms the worn and mottled metal of a manhole cover into a round wrecking ball using the Spherize filter. In addition to looking more realistic, this approach, he says, gives him more control over the look of the finished image. Spherize doesn't do the trick alone, though. You'll see how Lund adds shadows, highlights, and reflections from surrounding objects to heighten the illusion.

Step 1: Making round rounder

Lund starts by making a circular selection from the cropped image of the manhole cover. By holding down the Option/Alt-Shift keys while dragging with the Elliptical Marquee, he selects a perfect circle from the center (**Figure 11.1**). Then he opens the Spherize filter (Filter> Distort> Spherize) (**Figure 11.2**) and sets the Amount to 100 percent to get the maximum bulbous effect (**Figure 11.3**). The manhole cover now appears convex instead of flat.

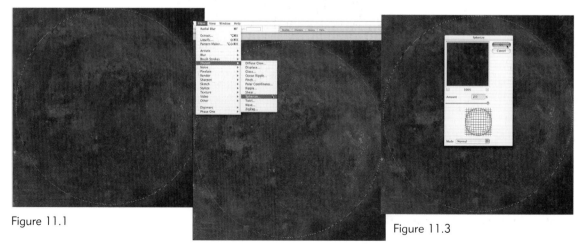

Figure 11.1

Figure 11.2

Figure 11.3

Step 2: Adding depth in context

Lund copies the ball, pastes it into the image of the sky and wall, and resizes it, positioning it close to the wall (**Figure 11.4**). He duplicates the ball layer and darkens it (Image> Adjustments> Brightness/Contrast) then creates a layer mask (Layer> Layer Mask> Hide All) (**Figure 11.5**). He paints in the darker layer around the lower perimeter of the wrecking ball (**Figure 11.6**), giving the illusion of more depth.

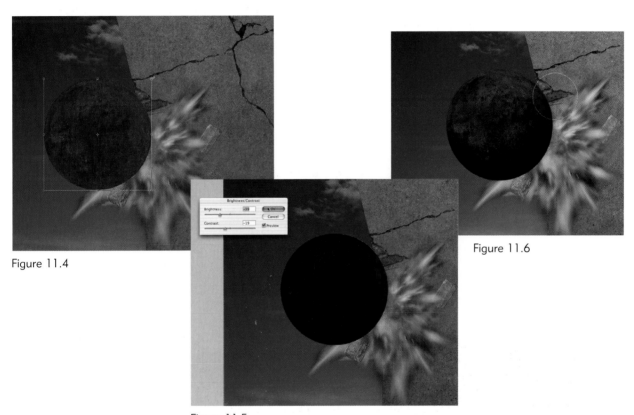

Figure 11.4

Figure 11.5

Figure 11.6

Step 3: Highlighting for curvature

You need more than shadows to produce dimension; you need highlights, too. To add the sun's reflection on the ball, Lund activates the lower wrecking ball layer and uses the Dodge tool to add a large, soft highlight. He sets the Exposure to 13 percent—the degree of lightness added by the Dodge tool—and alternates the Range between Highlights, Midtones, and Shadows until the reflection looks right (**Figure 11.7**).

He then links and merges the two wrecking ball layers (by clicking in the column to the left of the layer icon, then selecting Layer> Merge Linked) in preparation for painting with a layer mask that will make it appear as if the ball is immersed in the explosion. He creates a new layer mask for the ball (Layer> Add Layer Mask> Reveal All), and with a 400-pixel brush removes the ball's leading edge (**Figure 11.8**)—another way of adding the illusion of depth.

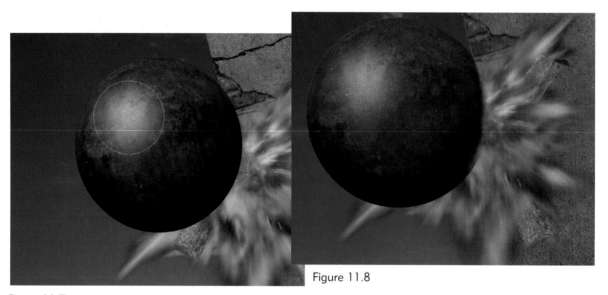

Figure 11.8

Figure 11.7

Step 4: Creating rounded reflections

To add the chain's shadow to the ball, Lund creates a new layer called Chain Shadow and locates it below the chain layer and above the wrecking ball layer. With a soft-edged brush of 135 pixels, he paints a black shadow on to the ball's surface (**Figure 11.9**). The smaller brush lets him mimic the ovoid links of the chain more accurately. He doesn't worry too much about being accurate—it's a shadow, after all.

Next, Lund uses the Eraser to form links by removing excess paint. He starts with a soft, small brush to form the links' interior (**Figure 11.10**) and then sets the brush at 473 pixels to thin the shadow's edges, which gives it perspective (**Figure 11.11**). He further refines the shadow's shape with the Smudge tool (using a variety of brush sizes) at Strength of 20 percent and Mode of Normal.

To finish the chain, he makes a new layer of the Chain Shadow and uses it to blend the junction of the ball and chain before merging the top chain layer with the top chain shadow layer (**Figure 11.12**). A few pushes of the Liquify brush to the chain and another round of motion blur finishes the wrecking ball (**Figure 11.13**). Bombs away!

Figure 11.9

Figure 11.10

Figure 11.11

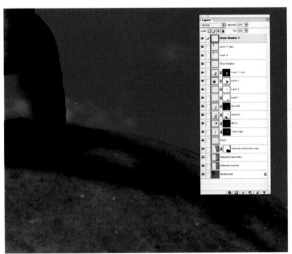

Figure 11.12

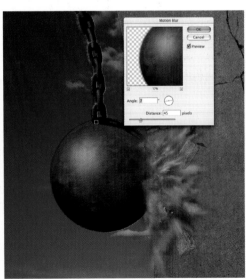

Figure 11.13

PART IV

Working with Color and Shadows

With the pieces in place and looking right, it's time to turn to the details—taking what's there and bringing it to the next level with the right color and shadows.

Details are one of Lund's fortes. His years of photographic experience give him an eye for nuance and color that comes from close observation of the world around him. While it may take years for casual photographers to develop a visual sense as acute as Lund's, the techniques he uses to incorporate his insights into his image are easily learned.

This section offers a peek at the kinds of things Lund looks for and the Photoshop techniques he uses to implement his vision. If you're expecting hard and fast rules, though, you won't find them here. "I have no formula for how to do this. For me it's always a matter of experimenting," Lund says.

Painting color into the exploding debris with basic brushes adds punch to an already dramatic image.

The Power of Color

The application or removal of color can punch up an image or subdue its mood. "Color can bring an image to life or it can take it over the edge," Lund says. "Luckily, with Photoshop we have the tools to create exactly the right color effect for an image."

"Crash Test Dummy" is a good example of how adding color to selected parts of an image can heighten its dramatic impact. The image itself—a multilayered composition of exploding computers and flying debris—is interesting and well made, but it lacks punch. Painting color into the explosion gives the image just the right amount of visual *oomph*.

Using Photoshop's paintbrushes to color an image is a relatively straight-forward process—pick a color, choose a brush, change its size—but it takes a few more steps to make painted-in color look natural. Playing with opacity levels and adjusting color intensity with Curves adds subtlety to the colored plumes of smoke.

Simple adjustments with the Hue/ Saturation controls and its Colorize option make an ordinary rooster exotic.

At the other extreme of how Lund adds color to an image is "Rooster." It's a very simple image—just a rooster composited against a sunrise. Indeed, the image would be nothing special if it weren't for the intense color Lund applies with Photoshop's Hue/Saturation controls. "With an image like 'Rooster,' using Photoshop to exaggerate color transforms an ordinary image into the extraordinary," Lund says. He notes with pride that "Rooster," one of his first Photoshop images from the early 1990s, remains a very popular stock image as this book goes to press.

The Secrets of Shadows

As we've seen in images like "Dominatrix" in Chapter 7, Lund pays a great deal of attention to the way light falls on an object, and the reflections and shadows the light creates. "Shadows are what separate the men from the boys," Lund says. "Bad shadows can ruin a composite, while well-done shadows can make a composite exquisite."

"Pool Dog" shows how shadows lend reality to an image. Anyone can tell that this image is an composite (unless they know a bloodhound trained to sip Mai Tais by the pool), but Lund's careful attention to the color, depth, and angle of shadows makes the image remarkably believable.

"When creating shadows there are many factors to take into consideration, such as the color of the shadow, its dimension, its falloff, and so forth," Lund says. "Leave any one of these important factors out, and the result will be a poor shadow. Most of all, you'll have a composite that just doesn't work."

In "Pool Dog," you'll see the many ways he creates shadows for different effects. "Making shadows requires a lot of tools and exploration," Lund says. "In some cases it might mean duplicating a layer, darkening it down, and using a layer mask, while in another case it might be a simple brush stroke." Lund creates his shadows on separate layers, so that he has the latitude to try different colors and opacities, shift shadows into the best positions, and adjust the shadows' colors.

The raft's shadow derived from the actual photo shoot, while the ball's and the dog's were added later. The angle and color of the raft shadow set the tone for the others.

With the image stripped away, these layers reveal the various colors and opacities Lund applied to shadows to get the best results.

Featured techniques
Painting with color
brushes

CHAPTER 12

Adding Impact with Color

'Crash Test Dummy' was actually the idea of *BYTE* art director Brian Day, who commissioned it for a computer magazine cover in the late 1990s. I later remade and embellished it for use as a stock image.

Putting together the original estimate for Brian, I found that renting a real crash test dummy would cost $3000—more than the entire budget for the finished cover. I remembered, though, that years ago I had shot such a dummy for an annual report. I found the images in my files. The photos were taken from the side, and the hands weren't visible. However, I thought the slides would still work.

The exploding parts came from a shoot I had done in the mid-1990s for yet another computer publication. In that case, we had contacted Survival Research Laboratories (SRL), a company that puts on pyro-technic displays. When we arrived at SRL, our contact greeted me with a handshake—which is when I noticed he was missing some fingers. He introduced me to his associate who was wearing an eye patch. I resolved to be very careful during our shoot.

Client: BYTE magazine, then r
published by Stone, a division

sh Test Dummy

Pick Up the Pieces

"Crash Test Dummy" is a good example of image recycling. The main components came from Lund's files: a mannequin from 1985 and explosions from the mid-1990s.

The crash test dummy was photographed at Failure Analysis Corporation in 1985 for its annual report. "I have to say that there is something unsettling about working with crash test dummies, especially when you see them out of the corner of your eye, just hanging around and watching you," says Lund. To make the photo more interesting, Lund added the scientific backdrop, assembled the machinery, and instructed the technician to play with wires. "Often as a photographer you walk into a photo shoot and there's nothing in the room. You need to find a way to add interest," he says. "People don't realize the degree of fabrication that goes on with traditional photography, as well as with a computer."

Because setting off actual explosions is illegal in San Francisco, Lund turned to Survival Research Laboratories, a company that builds machines, produces pyrotechnics, and makes performance art. SRL has built a reputation for creatively blowing things up, and this photo shoot was no exception. The SRL team filled soda cans with cement and then fired them from an air cannon at 500 feet per second, pulverizing the computer monitors—in a legal way. Lund remembers that the air cannon was fired by an SRL operative whose helmet was wired to the gun. "Wherever he turned his head, the cannon followed. For once in my life I didn't want to get someone's attention."

The computer and airbags were shot in the studio with a Leaf DCB attached to a Hasselblad medium-format camera. Lund constructed the airbags from a piece of cloth that's normally used with a fill reflector. He tied the material around a strobe-light head, whose fan inflated the material. For the second airbag, he made an indentation where the head would hit by setting up a light stand and attaching a pole that pushed into the material. "I shot two different airbags so that I would have alternatives," he says. "There is nothing worse than being in the middle of imaging and realizing you don't have the right parts."

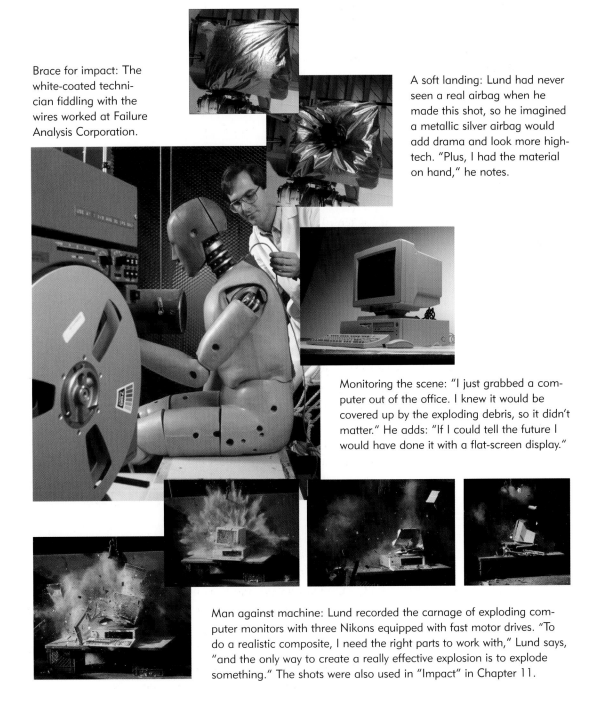

Brace for impact: The white-coated technician fiddling with the wires worked at Failure Analysis Corporation.

A soft landing: Lund had never seen a real airbag when he made this shot, so he imagined a metallic silver airbag would add drama and look more high-tech. "Plus, I had the material on hand," he notes.

Monitoring the scene: "I just grabbed a computer out of the office. I knew it would be covered up by the exploding debris, so it didn't matter." He adds: "If I could tell the future I would have done it with a flat-screen display."

Man against machine: Lund recorded the carnage of exploding computer monitors with three Nikons equipped with fast motor drives. "To do a realistic composite, I need the right parts to work with," Lund says, "and the only way to create a really effective explosion is to explode something." The shots were also used in "Impact" in Chapter 11.

Full Speed Ahead

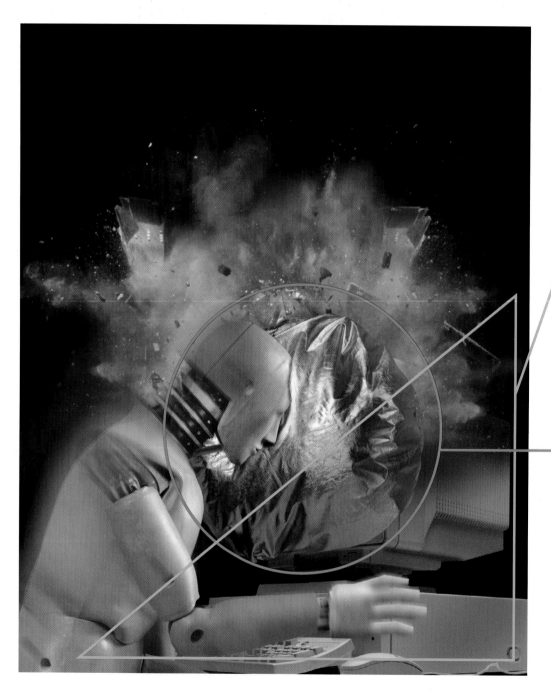

Lund selects the computer with the Pen tool, converts the path to a selection, and positions and sizes it in a new image, using Free Transform.

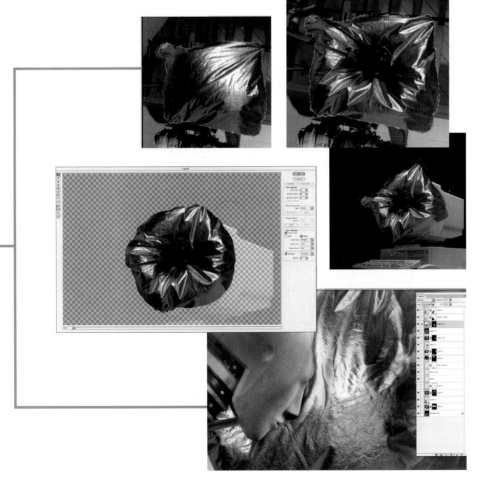

Lund selects the two airbags with the Pen tool. He pastes the first bag into the image of the computer, sizing and positioning it with Free Transform. To make the indented airbag look squishier, he uses the Liquify filter's Warp brush to push and pull it into a more rounded shape. He pastes the second airbag into the image, positions and sizes it with Free Transform, then uses the Liquify filter to emphasize a large crease near the bag's center to add to the impression that the dummy's head is pushing into the bag.

To blend the two bags together he makes a Hide All layer mask for the second bag and paints the crease back into place, blending it with the surrounding bag. Toward the end of the image composition process, he duplicates the dummy layer and places it at the top of the layer stack. Then he uses a layer mask to paint away the leading edge of the dummy's forehead so that the bag appears to be enveloping the head.

Four different shots of a computer being destroyed were painted together using layer masks.

Lund selects the crash test dummy with the Pen tool. He copies and pastes the selection into the main image, flips it horizontally, and then rotates, sizes, and positions it using Free Transform.

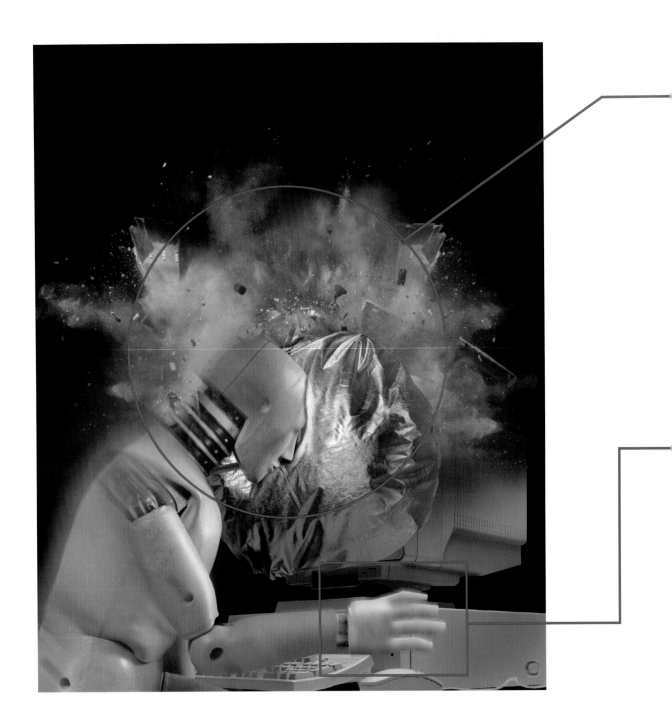

Lund adds color to the explosion by painting with an airbrush, its layer blend mode set to Color. He plays with its opacity and flow settings until he gets the desired effect.

THE LAYERS
How the image stacks up

Now Lund faces the real problem: "It becomes glaringly obvious that our dummy has no hand," Lund notes. He'll need to create one. He selects a patch of the forearm, then makes a new layer from the selection and extends the forearm with it. Using the Pen tool to make a path, he selects the shoulder joint and part of the upper arm and uses that selection to create a hand.

The fingers start with a rectangular piece selected with the Marquee tool. Lund makes a new layer for the new digit and duplicates it three times for a total of four fingers. He duplicates the fingers again, and rotates the new layers to curve the fingers slightly. He swipes the Burn tool along the underside of the fingers to give them dimension. Adding Motion Blur to the dummy's fingers and to the back (by adding Motion Blur to a new layer, which he paints in selectively with a layer mask) gives the impression of movement and speed. Blurring the hand also hides the patchwork nature of the new appendage.

Using Paint Tools to Add Color

Professional photographers like Lund are very careful to control the lighting in their shoots, but what's visible after the film is processed does not always have the desired impact. Sometimes, as in this case, a new color strategy is needed when the image is in a new context. That's when an artist like Lund turns into a painter. He uses Photoshop's paintbrushes to add color to pump up the drama or change the mood of an image. In "Crash Test Dummy," the contrast of the colorful explosion against the neutral-colored debris adds to its shock value.

Whether painting with color or blending in layer masks, Lund almost always uses the airbrush setting for his brushes—he likes the way it builds up its effect slowly. His choice of brush size is somewhat arbitrary, though—he just experiments with different sizes. Often he'll start out with the brush settings left over from a previous step. "I use whatever happens to be there, and if it proves to be less than effective, I change it," he says. Most of the time, it works just fine.

Step 1: Painting with explosions

Lund begins by creating a custom explosion—with layer masks rather than dynamite. "This is the fun part!" he says.

Figure 12.1

He opens the first monitor-explosion image and selects a part of the monitor frame with the Pen tool (**Figure 12.1**). He adds it to the main image that now includes the intact monitor, the airbag, and the dummy, which he has Pen-tooled, converted to a selection, and pasted into the image (**Figure 12.2**).

Adding a layer mask (Layer> Add Layer Mask> Reveal All), he paints away unnecessary portions of the monitor with a 308-pixel soft brush, switching to a smaller 55-pixel brush (in an 88-MB image) for the detail work. To make this new frame match the rest of monitor, he brings up Color Balance (Image> Adjustments> Color Balance) and nudges up the green level of that layer to +15 **(Figure 12.3).**

To add the first round of debris, he uses the Lasso tool to select a central portion of the first explosion image. He copies it, then pastes it and transforms it in the composite image (**Figure 12.4**). With another layer mask (Layer> Add Layer Mask> Hide All), he paints in the explosion with a 1242-pixel brush (**Figure 12.5**).

To get the proper sense of perspective, Lund shuffles layers. At this point, Lund sees that he has made a mistake: "I notice as I glance at my Layers palette that somewhere along the line I flattened the whole image. *Gulp!* It must have been when I was supposed to merge linked layers," he says. Flattening eliminates key layers and selections that he needs later in the process. "Well, let's continue and see how it goes!" he says. While not a complete disaster, this will mean more work, since he will have to repeat the process of selecting the dummy with the Pen tool. One consolation: Because it's his second time making the selection, it goes much faster. "When I remade it, I timed it: three-and-a-half minutes," he says with equal measures of chagrin and pride.

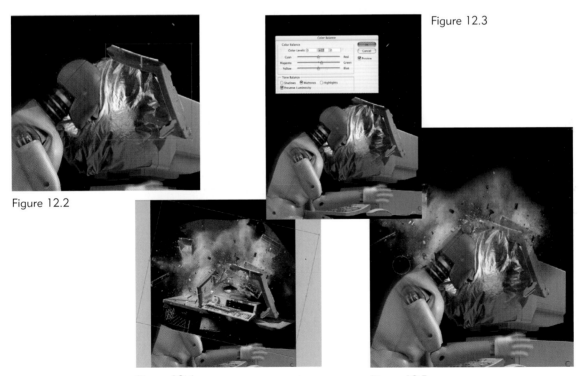

Figure 12.3

Figure 12.2

Figure 12.4

Figure 12.5

He clicks the background layer, then activates the Pen tool path he made of the dummy and turns the path into a selection again with a 1-pixel feather. He puts this new dummy layer just above the background layer, then sandwiches the explosion layer between them (**Figure 12.6**). The reshuffling yields a different emphasis on the exploding computer parts and changes the shape of the head.

More explosions are needed. He opens three more explosion images, copying and pasting them into the composite, adding layer masks (Layer> Add Layer Mask> Hide All), and then painting in the explosions with 442-pixel brushes **(Figure 12.7)**. All three (called Explode 3, Blow 2, and Blow 3, in Lund-speak) are transformed for position, angle, and orientation (**Figure 12.8**).

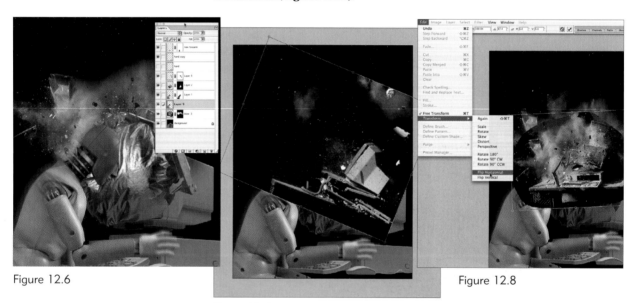

Figure 12.6

Figure 12.8

Figure 12.7

Lund "turns off" all the layers in the Layers palette except the background by clicking on the eye icons **(Figure 12.9)**. He selects the airbag from the background with the Pen tool and copies it into a new layer (Layer> New> Layer via Copy), then pastes in another explosion (**Figure 12.10**) and paints it in with a layer mask. Working with a layer for each image gives Lund flexibility in how the two images interact.

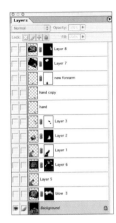

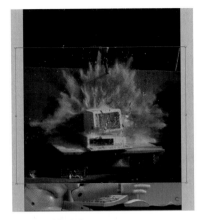

Figure 12.9   Figure 12.10

As a final touch, he uses the Burn tool (at 40% and set to Midtones), and with a 911-pixel soft brush adds a shadow from the explosion onto the computer on the background layer (**Figure 12.11**).

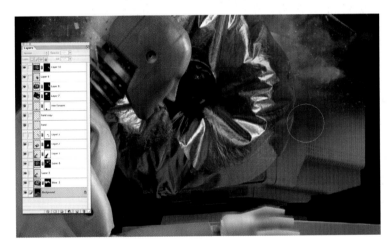

Figure 12.11

Step 2: Flattening layers—while keeping layers intact

He's fairly happy now with the shape of the explosion, but Lund wants to add color to the smoke and dust emanating out. The color that was right for the magazine cover won't do in this image—and it's a lot safer to add color in Photoshop than to try to create it in the midst of an explosion.

Lund simplifies the task even further by deciding to combine the explosion layers into a single layer, instead of coloring each layer individually. "I want to blend the colors in and out, play with opacity, and so on. Working on individual layers would quickly become a quagmire," he says.

Using the technique we saw in "Lighthouse" in Chapter 6, Lund creates a flattened version of the file in a new layer by creating a new layer at the top of the stack, and with the new layer selected, holding down the Option/Alt key and choosing Layer> Merge Visible.

Step 3: Painting with color

After all that preparation, the exploding debris can be imbued with flame-like colors of red and orange. He selects the paintbrush from the Toolbox, and in the Brush Options palette, clicks on the airbrush icon and makes a brush of about 1009 pixels, and chooses the Color blending mode. He picks a red color to simulate the fire of an explosion (Window> Color), dials down the opacity to 63% (**Figure 12.12**), and starts painting (**Figures 12.13** and **12.14**).

Figure 12.12

"Opacity can be used for a number of things," Lund says. "One use of transparency is to be able see enough through one element or layer so that you can clearly line parts up; the other is to create more subtlety in your composite, as I did here. I advise altering the opacities in your project just to see the effect—even if you're happy with something, try changing the opacity. You might yield even better results."

Painting, for Lund, is long on intuition and short on science. "It involves a lot of pressing Command-Z and going to the History palette to undo strokes and retrace my steps," he says. "I switch colors

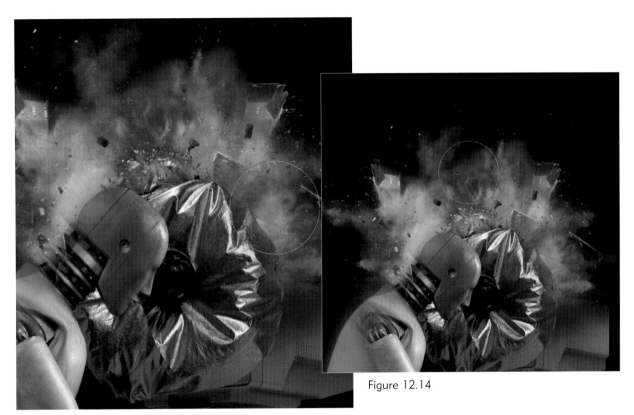

Figure 12.14

Figure 12.13

frequently and paint them in with varying degrees of overlap." Lund doesn't name or define his color swatches—he simply clicks on the color swatch in the Toolbox and uses Photoshop's color picker to choose his colors. "If the colors or overlays don't look right to me, I go back a couple of steps in the History palette and then try again with slightly different colors and amounts of overlap," he explains. The main thing, he says, is to trust your judgment and keep your fingers hovering over the Command/Ctrl-Z (Undo) keys.

Step 4: Touching up

Lund continues reordering layers and painting with layer masks to get the right sense of depth in the scene, such as making sure the dummy's forehead looks like it's being enveloped by the airbag. Lund moves the layer containing the blurred dummy to the top of the stack to accentuate the sense of motion **(Figure 12.15).**

Then it's time to look at the overall image for any fine-tuning. The dummy's head is a little dark, he sees. "I need to lighten it up and to introduce a little of the explosion's color," he notes. "For that matter, some of the color in the explosion looks a little too green." To take care of all of the color matters he chooses the airbrush, sets the mode to Color, the opacity to 50%, and the flow to 20%. Reducing the flow of the airbrush makes the paint build up at a slower rate, producing a more subtle effect. Choosing red for the foreground color, he paints red to bring the explosion's impact into the dummy and into the greenish parts of the explosion **(Figure 12.16).**

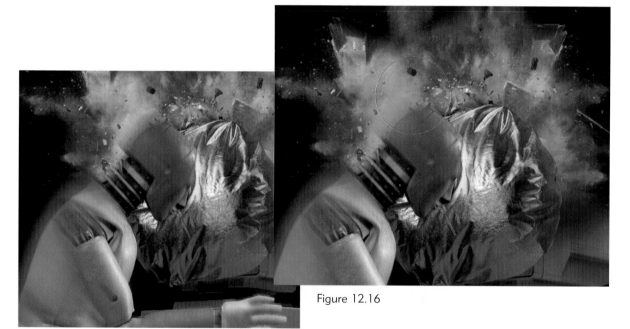

Figure 12.16

Figure 12.15

The final color tweak is to lighten up the dummy's head. First he checks to see that in the topmost dummy layer the head is the part that's visible through the layer mask (he doesn't want to lighten the whole dummy, just its head). It is, so he clicks on the image icon next to that layer (to ensure that he activates the image, not just the mask), then brings up Curves (Image> Adjustments> Curves) to lighten it **(Figure 12.17).** "Finally, or almost finally, there is an area of the air-bag just in front of the dummy's face that looks too gray," he notes. He uses a 140-pixel soft brush with the Clone tool on the airbag layer to fix that up **(Figure 12.18).** Safe at last.

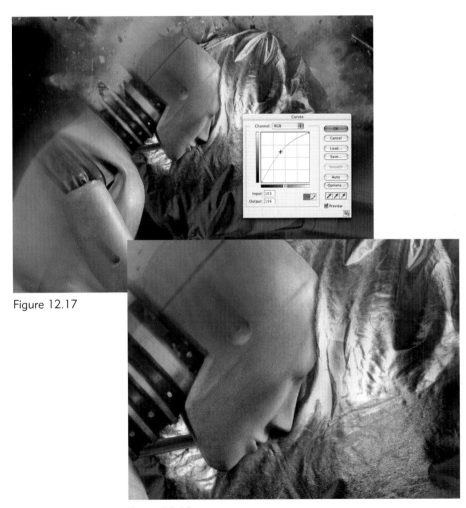

Figure 12.17

Figure 12.18

CHAPTER 13

Creating New Color Realities

"'Rooster' was one of my very first commercial Photoshop jobs. At the time I was totally strapped—that is, I had very little money and was having a difficult time paying my bills. I desperately wanted a larger monitor (I was using a standard 13-inch one). SuperMac was a company manufacturing and selling 21-inch monitors, which back then cost $5000 and required a $5000 video card to run efficiently.

I contacted SuperMac, showed them my Photoshop work, and struck a deal to create a colorful image, which they could then use to promote their equipment, in trade for a monitor and video card. 'Rooster' was the image that resulted.

Putting the image together was actually relatively simple—the kind of thing any novice could do with a couple of hours of Photoshop instruction. But back in the early 1990s, before Photoshop had the Pen tool, layers, and layer masks, it took me about a day and a half to get the image looking like I wanted. With today's tools it took me less than two hours."

Client: Originally, Super Mac Technologies; now a
stock photograph, published by Getty Images

Rooster

Something to Crow About

"The rooster was a shot from one of my very early days of assignment photography," Lund says. He's now an old hand at animal photography, but this was his first posed animal shot. "It was a job for a publication for farm children, the name of which I no longer remember. I do remember that it took about six months to get paid!"

The search for an appropriate rooster took him to a petting zoo in Oakland, California. According to Lund, the zookeeper chose the fowl that would be the model. "The selection was based not on appearance but on speed—whether or not she could catch it," Lund recalls. Once caught, the rooster was held by one of the zoo volunteers and photographed against a backdrop of foam core.

Lund remembers: "It was a typical summer day in the Bay Area—foggy—which turned out to be great for the composite. Harsh sunlight would not have fit in as well with the sunrise background." He shot the bird with a Nikon F2 camera.

He snapped the morning sky as the sun rose over his very first studio in San Francisco—at what is now left field of Pacific Bell Park, the baseball stadium in San Francisco. "I've had three studios and am in the process of building my dream studio on my property in Northern California," he says. It's a place where he's unlikely to get hit by a foul ball.

Morning has broken: Lund photographed the sunrise just outside his first studio in San Francisco.

Cock of the walk: Lund has since shot many chickens for his "Animal Antics" line of products, but he notes that one thing remains the same: "Chickens are disgusting."

Feeling Cocky

To bring the rooster into the sky, Lund first uses the Pen tool to create a new path. "I spent about 20 minutes trying to figure out the best way to select it," he says. "Then I just Pen-tooled it—and it took about 12 minutes to create the path." He converts it into a selection with a 2-pixel feather. After using Transform to position, size, and flip the image horizontally, he sees that a white outline is showing. He applies Defringe to the layer at a 1-pixel setting to change the white pixels to the color of the nearest nonbackground color. He adds a layer mask, and with a soft brush paints away some of the lighter fringing of some of the feathers.

Lund adds more dimension to the rooster with the Burn tool, darkening the undersides of the bird's comb and beak.

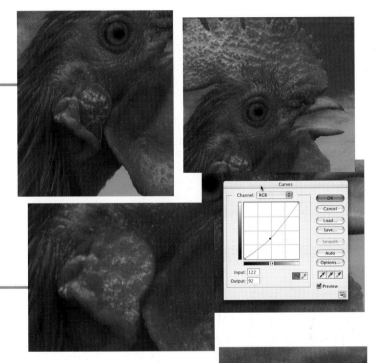

The rooster's cheek has some nasty-looking areas that need cleaning up. With the Lasso tool and a 12-pixel feather (extra feathering to create a looser edge to the change), he selects the cheek area. Now that its shape is defined, he drags the selection area to a part of the rooster's comb that doesn't have any obvious markings. He makes a new layer from that selection with the New Layer via Copy command. With the Move tool, he positions the new selection layer back over the cheek. Command/Ctrl-M brings up Curves, which he uses to slightly darken the new layer to more closely match the surrounding values. He uses a similar procedure to clean up the small patch of feathers just above and to the left of the area he just worked on.

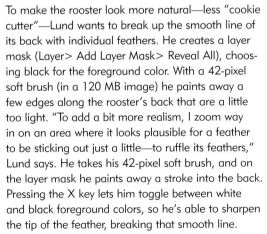

To make the rooster look more natural—less "cookie cutter"—Lund wants to break up the smooth line of its back with individual feathers. He creates a layer mask (Layer> Add Layer Mask> Reveal All), choosing black for the foreground color. With a 42-pixel soft brush (in a 120 MB image) he paints away a few edges along the rooster's back that are a little too light. "To add a bit more realism, I zoom way in on an area where it looks plausible for a feather to be sticking out just a little—to ruffle its feathers," Lund says. He takes his 42-pixel soft brush, and on the layer mask he paints away a stroke into the back. Pressing the X key lets him toggle between white and black foreground colors, so he's able to sharpen the tip of the feather, breaking that smooth line.

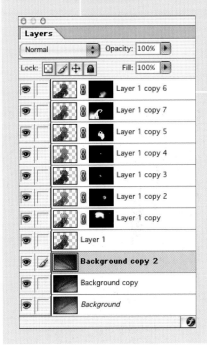

To add exotic coloring to a fairly drab bird, Lund merges the rooster layers, then duplicates the merged layers, selects the new layer, and opens Hue/Saturation. He sets it to Colorize, then moves the Hue/Saturation sliders to achieve the desired color effect. He then creates a layer mask and paints in the colored rooster where he wants the various colors to appear on the main bird. He does this six times—once for each color effect he uses. Each time, he creates a new layer, adjusts the color, then paints in the color with a layer mask.

With the colorizing of the rooster completed, Lund turns to the background image. He duplicates the sunset background and adjusts the Color Balance. The entire image is darkened with Curves. "Finally, I flip the background layer horizontally—it just looks better to me that way." he says. He realizes that he has now flipped *both* the rooster and the background. "Whatever works!" is his attitude.

Using Hue/Saturation to Create New Colors

In "Rooster," a drab barnyard rooster becomes an exotic bird through the use of Photoshop's Hue/Saturation controls. The key step here is checking the Colorize option, which replaces the image's original color with a single color. The colors pop off the screen, lending this everyday image an otherworldly aura.

"This is a reasonably easy color effect to make, but because it's so dramatic you need to exercise caution when applying it," Lund says. "I mostly use it when I'm working on monochromatic elements, for instance things that are—or that I want to be—pure red or pure blue." Lund used this technique to color the devil red in Chapter 8, "Reshaping Natural Elements," and here he uses it to add intense hues to seven different copies of the chicken. Each layer has different amounts of Hue/Saturation applied to it, but all have the Colorize option checked.

Once he's applied the bold colors, Lund tweaks them with Color Balance and Curves. The former lets him adjust the colors with a subtle hand, while the latter allows him to make changes in color density.

"Rooster" underscores Lund's Photoshop philosophy: Images do not need to be complicated or difficult to have impact.

Step 1: Setting the scene

After selecting the rooster with the Pen tool (**Figure 13.1**), Lund places it in the sunset scene, using Free Transform to size and flip it (Edit> Transform> Flip Horizontal). He ruffles its feathers to break up the smooth line of the back (**Figure 13.2**) and adds tiny feathers beneath the rooster's neck. He adds shadows to the underside of the feathers with the Burn tool and cleans up the bird's cheek.

The rooster is now ready for his more vibrant plumage.

Figure 13.1

Figure 13.2

Step 2: Creating new colors and painting them in

As always, Lund duplicates the layer he's about to work on—in this case, the rooster layer. With the layer now selected, he goes to Image> Adjustments> Hue/Saturation and clicks the Colorize button. Lund has an idea of the colors he thinks would work, but he doesn't have an exact formula for each color. "I move the sliders around until I see what I like," he says. He slides Hue to 44, Saturation to 100, and leaves lightness at 0 to create a bright yellow (**Figure 13.3**). He creates a layer mask (Layer> Add Layer Mask> Hide All), and with a large (618-pixel) soft brush paints the comb back in to the main rooster (**Figure 13.4**).

Figure 13.3

Figure 13.4

When the bright new comb is fully painted in, he goes to Image> Adjustments> Brightness/Contrast and sets the Brightness to –27 and the Contrast to +38 to increase the intensity of the color (**Figure 13.5**). In this case, Lund doesn't use adjustment layers, which would let him confine color to a specific area. Rather, he uses image adjustments to the entire layer. One reason for taking this approach is that he can use the same selection seven times, making it easier to "paint inside the lines"—a benefit, given all those tiny feathers. But most of all, by keeping separate layers and painting them together using layer masks, he can decide on the fly how much of each color to show in which areas. "It really seemed like the most efficient way to do it," he says.

He repeats this process, using different Hue/Saturation variations seven times, each time painting in an area of color using layer masks and then adjusting the Brightness/Contrast. He creates a bright red for the head, orange for the beak, brighter red and purple for the wattles, green for the iris, and so on (**Figure 13.6**).

Figure 13.5

Figure 13.6

Step 3: Toning it down

Although Lund wants a brightly colored bird, he admits the rooster is looking a bit implausible at this stage, so he activates the layer that contains the color mask for most of the rooster's body and feathers and opens Hue/Saturation again. Dropping Saturation back down to –36 (Colorize *un*checked) gives him the look he wants (**Figure 13.7**).

Figure 13.7

Step 4: Brightening the sunset

Such a brightly colored bird makes even the sunset look bland, so Lund duplicates the background layer and opens Color Balance (Image> Adjustments> Color Balance). As Lund looks at the image, he recognizes that it has a broad range of tones, so he concentrates his adjustments in the midtones. "I just do it by eye," he says. "If an image is primarily light in nature, it'll mostly be affected by adjusting the highlights; if it's got a lot of dark areas, work on the shadows."

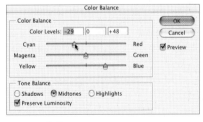

Figure 13.8

So in Color Balance, with Tone Balance set to Midtones, he moves the top slider toward Cyan (-29). The middle slider stays at 0, and the bottom slider moves toward Blue (+48) (**Figure 13.8**).

"Sometimes it's hard to decide which tonal range to use," Lund says. "In that case, I dive in and start with the midtones and then see what happens. After that, I try highlights and/or shadows until it looks right to me." Lund says, too, that during these tonal adjustments, he frequently zooms in to 100% to make sure the image is not becoming too grainy or losing detail as a result of his manipulations. He also looks for *banding,* in which there are stripes of color caused by the loss of gradations between colors.

Once the Midtones (or Highlights or Shadows) settings have been adjusted, Lund pulls down the Curves a bit to slightly subdue the image colors (**Figure 13.9**). "With Curves I work on the color density—that is, I lighten or darken it. I can also use it to adjust the contrast by creating more of an *S* curve," he says, referring to the shape of the graph in the dialog box in which Curves are adjusted. "I also have the flexibility to anchor the curve with control points and limit the tonal movements between those points." He chuckles: "I'm sure some other books can explain how this works better than I can. I just know what looks right." (Some of those helpful books are listed in the Resources section at the back of this book.)

Figure 13.9

Step 5: Flipping the background

Finally, Lund thinks the image scene will have more impact if the background is flipped. He duplicates the sky layer ("more from force of habit than any real need," says Lund) and flips it (Edit> Transform> Flip Horizontal). Now the rooster appears to be backlit by the morning sun's rays (**Figure 13.10**).

Good morning!

Figure 13.10

Featured techniques
  Layer masks
  Eyedropper
  Smudge tool
  Opacity

CHAPTER 14

Casting Shadows

"'Pool Dog' started as a sketch given to me by my 'handler'—Collette Carter, senior art director at Portal Publications, which publishes my 'Animal Antics' line of greeting cards.

The first step of bringing the idea into a photographic reality was to photograph our heroine, a bloodhound named Scarlett provided by Bow Wow Productions. Ever tried to get a bloodhound to lie on its back? Well, I don't know about every bloodhound, but Scarlett was not interested, and bloodhounds are big dogs! It wasn't that she was hostile or anything like that. Rather that she simply wouldn't lie on her back without losing her doleful expression. In order to create an image that looked like she was lounging in the pool, I would have to modify my approach. I built a platform in my studio with plywood and a couple of sawhorses. The animal trainer stood on the platform, holding Scarlett in a standing position.

After finishing with Scarlett in the studio, I headed to the pool. I like to think of this completed image as a future self-portrait. "

Pool Dog

Nothin' but a Hound Dog

"Bloodhounds always look so blasé, which seems like a perfect expression for a dog relaxing in the pool," Lund says.

Taking shots like the ones in "Pool Dog" requires a lot of advance planning. Lund knew that he would be modifying the images in Photoshop, so he factored the final composite into his thinking. "I knew that I'd need to rotate Scarlett's body to look like she was lying on her back on the raft, so I set up the studio lights with that in mind," Lund says. He made sure the lighting hit the dog from the same angle as it would when the dog "rolled over" in Photoshop and that it mimicked the angle of the sun shining on the raft at the pool.

To get the right angle for the composite, the handler put Scarlett on a platform so Lund could shoot her belly from below. The lighting was angled up and to the right. It should be noted that the animal was not harmed during Lund's photo shoot, and Lund refuses to work with handlers whom he feels are too rough with their animals.

The shoulders, paws, and head were all photographed separately. "One of the tricky parts of this kind of work is guessing ahead of time about exactly what parts will be needed and from what angles, so I always shoot more than I need," Lund notes. All of the photography was done with a Hasselblad camera using Kodak E100S film.

Good libations: Have to get the umbrella drink in! In addition to capturing the overall scene, Lund shot the props individually in case he needed the alternate angles.

Smile!: Please...?

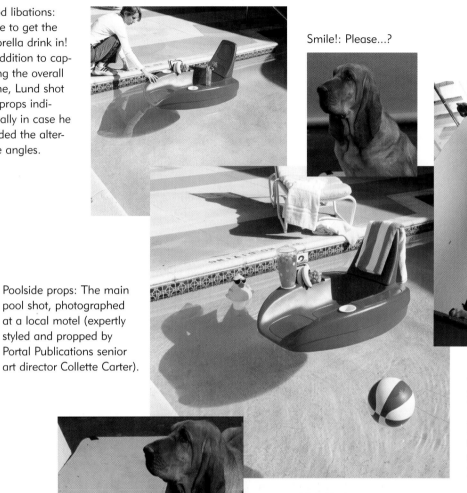

Poolside props: The main pool shot, photographed at a local motel (expertly styled and propped by Portal Publications senior art director Collette Carter).

Frankly, Miss Scarlett: "Bloodhounds are big, heavy, drooling machines!" Lund says. Since bloodhounds don't happily lie on their backs, the trainer had to hold Scarlett upright, looking, somehow, relaxed.

The paws that refreshes: This pose was for the arm that cups the drink.

Just relax: The shot that was used to put an arm across the bloodhound's belly.

Oh, You Dawg

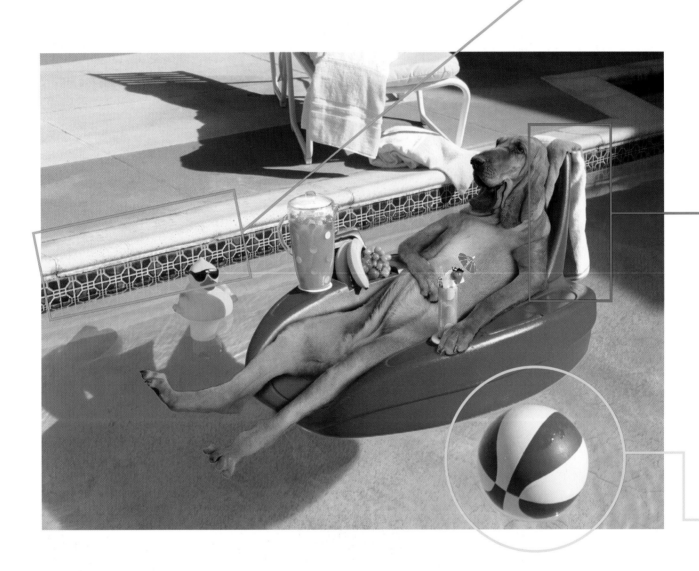

To remove unwanted lettering on the pool deck, Lund simply uses the Polygonal Lasso tool to select the area marked by letters. He drags the Marquee to a clean area of deck. Then holding the Command/Ctrl and Option/Alt keys, he drags the clean selection back to the area he wants to cover up.

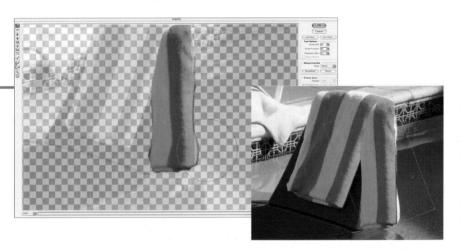

The highlights on the white towel were blown out (without enough detail). To correct that, Lund selects a better-exposed part of the towel with the Pen tool, converts the path to a selection, and the selection to a layer. He uses Transform to reposition the newly created layer and the Liquify filter set to Warp to reshape the towel to fit over the previous one. Excess towel is removed with the help of a layer mask.

The beach ball is too far away from the raft. Lund moves it closer by selecting the ball and a large area around it with the Lasso tool. He converts the selection to a layer and moves it into its new position. With a layer mask and a large, soft brush, he paints away some of the new layer, blending the two layers together until the water's ripples and other details seem realistic.

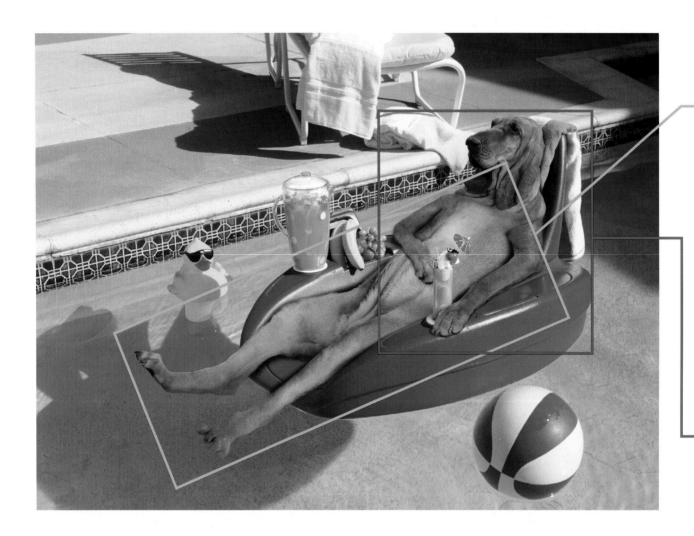

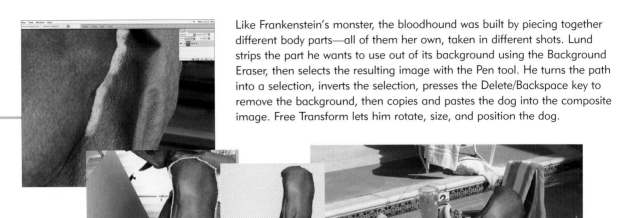

Like Frankenstein's monster, the bloodhound was built by piecing together different body parts—all of them her own, taken in different shots. Lund strips the part he wants to use out of its background using the Background Eraser, then selects the resulting image with the Pen tool. He turns the path into a selection, inverts the selection, presses the Delete/Backspace key to remove the background, then copies and pastes the dog into the composite image. Free Transform lets him rotate, size, and position the dog.

Lund uses the same techniques to isolate the dog's head and "arms." He converts the paths to selections, then copies, pastes, and positions the arms and head in the composite image. The Liquify filter gives the arms the right curves, especially the paw draped over her belly. Lund places the selected head on the body, setting the opacity to 60% to better see placement, then joins the dog's head to its body again using a layer mask set to Reveal All. Brushing over the layer mask, he blends the images, then moves the order of the layers so that the head layer is below the body layer. Last, he brushes out excess bits of the body and the arm.

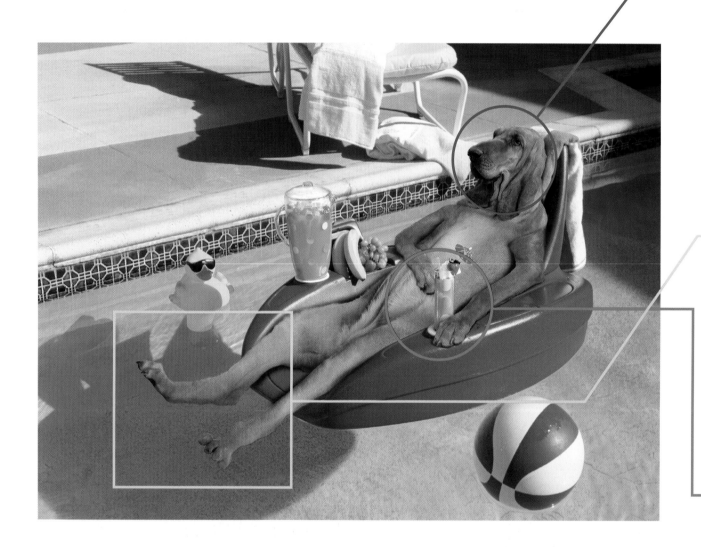

A dour bloodhound just won't do. Lund puts a mile on Scarlett's face with one push of the Liquify brush.

Lund uses a layer mask painted with gray to make the legs appear semi-transparent—or underwater.

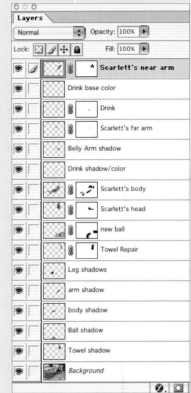

THE LAYERS

How the layers stack up

The dog's toes are flattened—remember she was standing on her hind legs—so Lund uses the Liquify filter to push the toes out to look fuller and rounder.

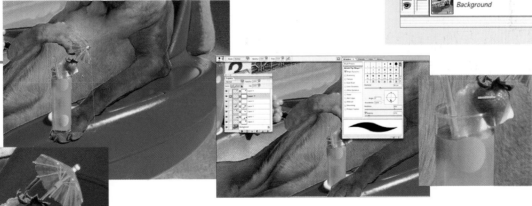

With the Pen tool, Lund selects the drink and uses Transform to position and size it. Making a layer mask for the drink, he paints the glass into the cup holder. He sets the foreground color to gray and paints on the glass's mask. In masks, remember, gray provides translucency, so by painting on the mask with gray, the glass becomes transparent, and the dog's fur is visible through it.

Adding Shadows with Layer Masks

To truly mimic the look of traditional photography—and thus to add to a digital composite's verisimilitude—maintaining consistent lighting is paramount. And consistent lighting casts consistent shadows. As we've seen throughout this book, Lund pays a great deal of attention to the shadows in his images. He routinely adds shading to objects, making sure that dark areas line up with the light source he's captured on film or that he's imagined in his mind's eye.

"Pool Dog" is an interesting exercise in creating shadows, in that the central figure—the bloodhound—is made of numerous parts, each of which needs shadows applied to it. The outdoor scene was shot on a sunny day, so the chaise longue's real shadow on the bottom of the pool can be used as a reference point to align the pseudo shadows.

An important aspect of adding realistic-looking shadows is keeping in mind not only the direction of the light, but also how it works with the colors in the picture. "Shadows are not usually totally black," Lund notes. "They have color in them. The color of the shadow is a combination of the color of the underlying area and the color of the light being reflected back into the area that's covered by the shadow." Lund uses sharp eyes and sampling to get the proper hues.

Step 1: Creating the body's shadow

After the lounging hound is assembled, Lund turns to the shadows. It's those touches of startling realism that will make viewers believe for at least a moment that the dog is actually spending the day poolside.

Lund creates a new layer labeled "body shadow" (Layer> New> Layer). He places that layer just above the background layer (**Figure 14.1**). He sets up a 176-pixel brush (in a 61-MB image) with a hardness of 75% (**Figure 14.2**). He also temporarily sets the opacity of the body layer to 70% so he can better see where to place the shadow underneath (**Figure 14.3**).

Figure 14.1

Figure 14.2

Figure 14.3

Lund uses a firmer brush here, because the sunlight overhead would create hard-edged shadows. "Shadows are hard-edged in harsh light, and soft-edged in subdued light. Shadows also get softer and lighter as they get further away from the light source," Lund explains. "As the shadow gets further from the object casting it, more ambient light fills in the shadow, making the overall effect lighter."

"To create truly realistic-looking shadows, it helps to look at real shadows," Lund advises. Then, reassuringly, "A shadow can be very effective without being totally accurate—as long as it has enough of the real characteristics like color, edge, and angle."

Step 2: Finding the right color

When making shadows, you can often quickly get the right color by selecting from colors already in the image that appear under similar lighting conditions. In this case, he works on the assumption that the dog's fake shadow would have characteristics similar to the raft's real shadow. Lund uses the Eyedropper tool to sample a dark blue from an existing shadow on the raft, then uses that color when brushing along the contour of the dog's far side (**Figure 14.4**).

Now for the first arm's shadow. This shadow should be a bit darker, as it is above the body shadow. He creates a new layer titled "arm shadow" just above the previous layer. With the same brush and color settings, and an opacity of 79% (to adjust the darkness), he lays down a shadow underneath the arm in the foreground (**Figure 14.5**). He uses the Eraser (189-pixel brush) to soften the shadow at the end of the paw (**Figure 14.6**). Again, Lund uses the real shadow cast by the chair and other pool props to guide his placement of the shadows cast by the dog. Adjusting the shadow's opacity in small increments lets him fine-tune its density to keep it the same color range as the body shadow but also to darken it slightly.

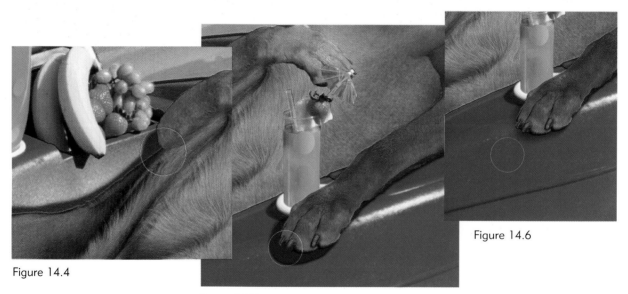

Figure 14.4

Figure 14.5

Figure 14.6

Step 3: Smudging the shadow

With the same brush, but now with the Smudge tool selected, Lund lengthens the paw shadow and pushes in the shadow under the elbow (**Figure 14.7**). "The key to the Smudge tool is its icon—a finger being drawn across the surface. It's great for just pushing a shadow into a slightly better position," Lund says. "It's easier to control than an eraser or even an airbrush."

Step 4: Noting the contours

Lund makes a shadow layer for the legs using the same brush settings as he did when adding shadows to the body but with the opacity set to 70% (**Figure 14.8**). He darkens the area between the dog's legs, where its haunch would cast a larger shadow. A 257-pixel soft-edged brush then adds a bit more soft shadow at the bottom of the dog's near leg (**Figure 14.9**).

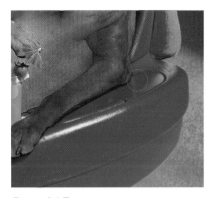

Figure 14.7

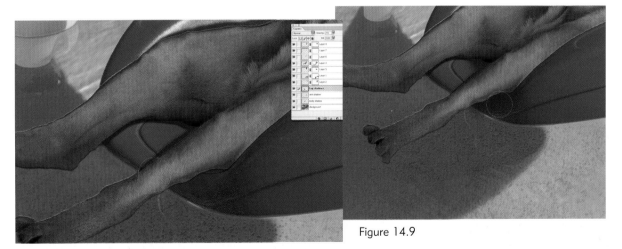

Figure 14.9

Figure 14.8

Step 5: Sampling shadows

For the shadow cast by the arm slung across the belly, Lund knows the light is different—the shadow is falling on fur rather than the raft. He uses the Eyedropper tool to sample a dark shadow from beneath the ear. In this case, the dog's fur would be the primary agent controlling the shadow's color.

Now he creates a new layer ("belly arm shadow") and moves it in the layer stack to just below the layer of its corresponding arm. With a layer opacity of 90% and a 70-pixel, 50% hard brush, Lund paints in the shadow below the arm, again seeking to mimic the lighting conditions (**Figure 14.10**). As with the first arm, he softens the shadow under the paw. Then he paints a shadow under the dog's upper arm (**Figure 14.11**).

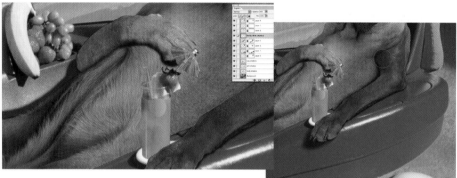

Figure 14.10

Figure 14.11

Step 6: Adding dimension to shadows

To refine the shadow areas, Lund uses the Burn tool on the dog body layer, running it several times along the seam where the body meets the raft. He does this first with Range set to Midtones, and then again with Range set to Highlights (**Figure 14.12**).

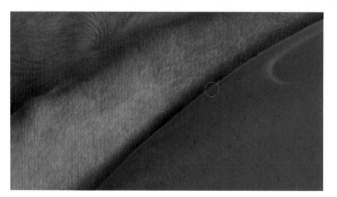

Figure 14.12

In this case, as in most cases when using Dodge (which lightens pixels) and Burn (which darkens them), Lund starts with Midtones then switches to Highlights and Shadows while closely observing the results. "I use Command-Z [Control-Z for Windows]a lot!" Lund explains. "This is very much a process where there is no substitute for seeing the results and adjusting one's approach appropriately. Each image reacts a little differently depending on its own color mix, brightness, contrast, and tonal range."

Step 7: Depicting light reflected through color

Not all shadows are dark. Some, like the light cast through a bright, transparent color like the pink drink, are actually lighter than what they fall on. The desired effect is less shadow than cast light. Therefore, it needs to be lighter and more transparent than a typical shadow.

To make it appear as if light is shining through the pink drink, Lund creates a new layer (Mode: Color, Opacity: 60%) and uses the color picker to set the foreground color to a pink sampled from the liquid in the glass. With a 100-pixel brush, he paints pink onto the raft and body (**Figure 14.13**).

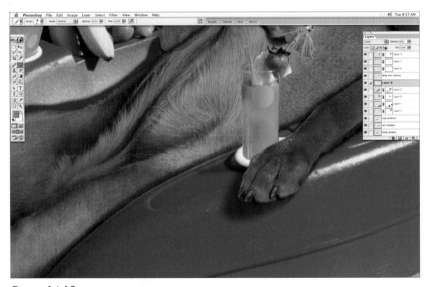

Figure 14.13

Step 8: Making a shadow seem like it's underwater

The final touches include casting the beach ball's shadow on to the bottom of the pool by using the elliptical Marquee tool to drag out an oval that seems about the right size and shape and by positioning it over the existing shadow (of the raft) on the bottom of the pool. He gives it a soft feather of 22 pixels to make it appear diffused by the water, then presses Command/Ctrl-J to create a new layer from the selection. He drags this new layer into position with the Move tool (**Figure 14.14**). Now this layer holds a shadow with the same coloration as the raft's shadow but in the size and shape of the beachball.

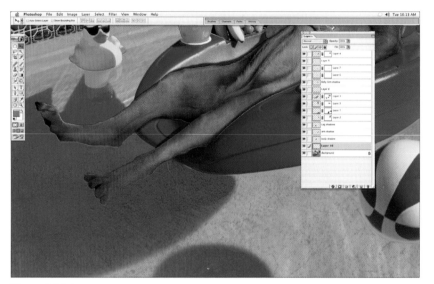

Figure 14.14

Lund adds the shadow the dog's head would cast on the beach towel by first making a new layer just above the background layer, selecting a shadow color with the Eyedropper (he picks the color under the ear again), and paints the color in, using a large, soft brush (**Figure 14.15**).

For a final look at all the shadows, Lund turns off all the other layers (**Figure 14.16**). Now the colors and edges of the different shadows are plainly visible. See the light?

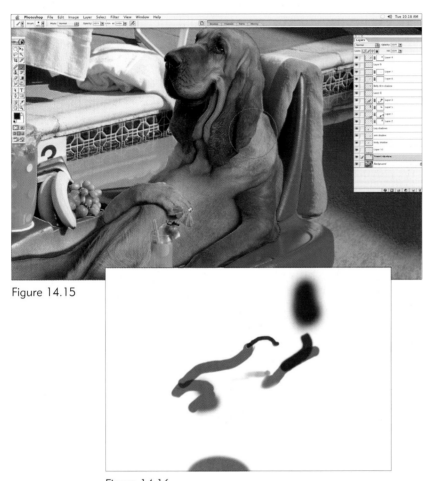

Figure 14.15

Figure 14.16

With a career that spans nearly a quarter century, John Lund has thousands of compelling images in his archives, many of which resurface in his digital composites. While the techniques described in the preceding chapters apply to the images that follow, the stories behind them are unique. Here are more examples of Lund's remarkable vision and inimitable personality.

PART V

Gallery

Ascent

Client: Stock photograph, published by Corbis

I first met the model Lisa Lowe when I hired her as a makeup artist. In addition to her cheerful and upbeat attitude, I noticed she had
exceptional biceps. I discovered that her primary interest is fitness,
so I decided to photograph her in a way that showed off her physical
condition—and generate some income for me! An image that illustrated
determination, perseverance, strength, and courage in the face of over-
whelming odds would do the trick.

I mulled the shot over for quite some time before the rope idea came to
me. It fit all of my criteria: Dramatic, relatively easy to do, and very little expense. I hung the rope from the ceiling of my studio and had Lisa
sit on a stool as I shot from above. She grabbed the rope and assumed
a pose emulating an actual climb. We tried a number of slight variations
and different facial expressions. My assistant sprayed her with water
from a spray bottle to give the impression of perspiration, particularly
where her hair met her forehead. I wanted it to look like she was really
working. I ended up using five different shots of her, compositing them
together to get the best-looking pose, facial expression, and hair.

Next we photographed the rope alone. The final building block was a
sky that I had photographed years earlier in Santa Fe. In one shot there
was a hole in the clouds. When I inverted the clouds and rotated them
180 degrees, it left the impression that we were looking down through
a hole in the clouds rather than up through a hole. The Liquify brush
added ripples to the rope.

When I finished the image I sent it to one of my stock agencies,
which promptly rejected it. "What can I do to make it work?" I asked.
"Nothing," was the reply; it just doesn't work. I sent the image to a second agency I work with. The people there loved it, ran the image full-
bleed in their next catalog, and selected it to represent the agency in a
juried exhibition. Perseverance in action! The best part, though, is that
it sells and sells and sells.

Bar Code

Client: Stock photograph, published by Corbis

One of the popular and timeless themes of stock photography is *standing out from the crowd.* A bar code represents conformity and loss of identity, so it seemed a perfect subject. But what to do with it? While staring for some time at a bar code, I saw that the lines actually looked like the bars of a jail cell. I could have someone imprisoned behind them—better yet, I could have someone escaping from them!

I had recently worked with Barbara, a beautiful woman of Asian descent who sports a shaved head, giving her a futuristic look (that's Barbara in "Tech Woman" in Chapter 9). She had also worked with several other photographers I know, and at least two of them had taken some great shots of her screaming. I liked the idea of her screaming in frustration as she bent the bars apart in her escape attempt. I gave her a call and asked her to bring some clothes of a timeless nature. After a slight pause she suggested, "Why don't I be nude—those are my favorite shots anyway." Who was I to object?

This image is stark evidence of how simple an effective image can be. Barbara positioned her hands as if she were prying bars apart and simulated a scream. I photographed a bar code and scanned it in. With Barbara on a layer beneath the bar code as a guide, I used the Liquify brush to nudge the bars apart. *Ta-da!* A fast, inexpensive image that is a clear, quick read—in other words, my favorite kind.

Cat & Canary

Client: Stock photograph, published by Getty Images

This image certainly did not live up to my expectations, but it did change my life and start a whole new career. The idea behind it was a business concept: a humorous image depicting victory, slyness, or the rewards of a clever plan. I began with a friend's kitten. I set up a single strobe light in my friend's living room and, with a fill reflector, shot the kitten while it was on her lap. At home I procured an escapee from my feather pillow. I reshaped the kitten's face into a smile with the Liquify brush.

I mentioned that this image changed my life. I reserved the paper product rights to it, then sent it off to my stock agency. It has never done particularly well as a stock image—only about a half-dozen sales in four years. I did, however, make an appointment with an art director at a publishing company that produces greeting cards, among other things. I showed her the image and suggested that we do a line of similar humorous animal images. To my eternal surprise she agreed. That was four years ago, and now the 'Animal Antics' greeting cards provide a good portion of my income."

How did this image change my life? I now know far more about cats and dogs than I would ever have imagined. Better yet, I know just exactly how a *cat who swallowed the canary* feels.

Cloverleaf

Client: Stock photograph, published by Getty Images

I am always trying to come up with interesting and dramatic ways to depict the technological advances sweeping over us. Communications, in particular, is one of the hottest categories in stock imagery. In trying to come up with an image that would apply to communications in general, and networking specifically, it occurred to me that a freeway might make a great illustration. A cloverleaf in particular would be a good representation of a network. But how to use my digital capabilities to take the image beyond the ordinary?

The answer, for me, was in creating the most complicated, complex cloverleaf ever. All I would need is a couple of overhead shots of existing freeway interchanges. The opportunity came during an assignment to shoot the Golden Gate Bridge from a helicopter. En route we passed over a freeway interchange near the Bay Bridge, and I had the pilot fly a few tight turns over it. When making such turns, helicopters bank just as a plane would, giving me a straight-down shot, clear of such impediments as landing struts and so forth. I've done this enough times— including for the shoot that resulted in "Circuit City" in Chapter 5—to know that as long as I am looking through a camera I am fine, but if I stop looking through the camera I quickly begin to get airsick.

Back at the studio, I selected various roadways and repositioned them in an ever more complex cloverleaf. But while it looked appropriately complicated, it didn't look real. I tried inverting the images. It worked. Suddenly the different shadow angles and subtleties that had worked against me didn't matter anymore. Not only did the details no longer detract from the image, but inverting the image and changing the Hue and Saturation made it more abstract and better as a conceptual piece.

The roadways had actually been pretty empty at the time I made the original shot, so I finished up by silhouetting some of the vehicles and copying them until we had a sufficient vehicular density.

Deer in the Headlights

Client: Stock photograph, published by Getty Images

Clichés can be good stock ideas. *A deer caught in the headlights* is one such example. It's a good metaphor for a time of rapid technological change. It's the way I often feel myself.

I called Bow Wow Productions, the animal trainers that I have turned to so often, and asked whether they could get me a deer. No problem. I rejected the idea of actually photographing the deer on location. There were too many potential pitfalls—permits, a road to be cordoned off, a short shooting window in regard to the light (we would need to shoot after sunset but before the sky lost its color). What if the deer bolted? It had to be a studio shot.

When the deer arrived at our studio, the first thing the trainer said to me was "Whatever you do, don't get her flight-reflex going!" Her flight-reflex? I had visions of the deer bounding off the walls of my studio amid crashing light stands and exploding power packs. I asked if the strobe flash might cause such a reflex. "Don't know," was the answer.

The backdrop I chose was dark blue, as I envisioned the deer in the dark blue of twilight. It's always best to use a backdrop that closely matches the background color of your composite. Then I placed two strobe heads on either side of my tripod-mounted camera to simulate a pair of headlights. In order to avoid "flight-reflex" problems, we started with the power on the lowest setting and the deer happily munching from a bowl of grain on the studio floor. First pop: no reaction. Increase the power and fire another flash. Again, no problem. Actually the only problem was getting the deer to be attentive to the camera. We ended up clapping, yelling, whistling, and generally making a huge commotion to get the deer to pop her head up and look in our direction.

With the deer photographed, I turned to the background. I went up to Sonoma County in Northern California, where a friend lives off of a long, narrow, winding asphalt private road. At dusk I positioned my truck on the right side of the road and set up my camera between the headlights illuminating the road in front of me. I then bracketed my exposures frantically as the twilight turned to darkness.

In Photoshop, I widened the road and darkened the background, before
pasting the deer into it. The scene looked a little too static. If someone
had managed to get this shot in reality, there would probably be some
movement as the flash fired and froze the deer, but the shutter speed
would show some camera movement during the exposure. I fixed that
by pasting in the deer several times to simulate a slight blur of movement. The image sells well, and everyone, even those who know that
everything I do is digital, is surprised when they find out I shot the deer
in the studio.

Fighting Fire

Client: Stock photograph, published by Getty Images

I was sorting through some old slides when I came across some shots I had taken of a burning building. A shot of firemen at work seemed like a good idea for a stock image, but of course I wanted a twist. *Fighting fire with fire* popped into my brain.

I arranged to rent firemen's garb, and my assistant coaxed a friend of his into modeling. We lit the "fireman" by bouncing a strobe light, colored with a light-orange gel, off of a 4-by-8-foot sheet of white foam core. I used a second sheet of foam core behind the model's back to bounce in fill light.

I found another slide in my files of smoke from a burning field. Using a layer mask, I blended the smoke image and the fire image into a single background.

Now I needed the flame. When I was very young, a bunch of us kids used to hold matches or candles up to cans of spray paint to create our own "flame throwers." The scariest part was the chance that the flame could be drawn back into the can and blow it up. In creating "Fighting Fire" (and "Dragon"), I used that technique to get the flame that emerges from the fire hose. In my determination to get the shot I held that spray can button down a *looonnnng* time. In fact, I held it down so long that the whole can caught on fire—but no explosion!

I sent the image off to the stock agency. They liked it, but they wanted the fireman to be wearing a face shield. That meant re-shooting the fireman—or did it? I decided to try improvising the face shield to spare the expense and hassle of reshooting. I drew the outline of a face shield with the Pen tool and created a path that I turned into a selection and filled with varying shades of orange.

Rescue

Client: Stock photograph, published by Stone, a division of Getty Images

Businesses often try to communicate the message that they can rescue their clients from one sort of a problem or another, so I set out to create a stock image to convey that idea in a clear and striking way. Of course, I also wanted it to honor my usual criteria that images should be inexpensive to make, relatively easy to create, and fun to do.

A life preserver would be a good symbol for the image, but I needed drama—a storm at sea and a life preserver being thrown into it. The idea of heading out to sea during a storm so that I could get my stock image was unappealing on at least two counts: I easily get seasick and I'm chicken. The answer was to create my own storm. I used these same waves, shot at the Cliff House in San Francisco, later for "Lighthouse" (Chapter 6).

Now I needed the life preserver. Renting one from a local prop house, I photographed it in the studio. To get slightly directional but soft and diffuse lighting to match that of the foggy day near the Cliff House, I bounced strobes off of the ceiling. I tied a rope between two columns and photographed that with the same lighting. Both images were captured using the Leaf digital camera back I mounted on a Hasselblad ELM camera.

The technique I used to composite the waves is essentially the same as described in "Lighthouse": painting 10 waves together using layer masks. To create a stormy sea scene in this way takes me about six hours or so to get it looking the way I want, but even though I'm using the same parts I've used before, I don't want them to look like the same thing. Each image, each situation, is different. I then Pen-tooled the life preserver and the rope, and copied and pasted them into place. I used the Liquify brush to push the rope into a more curved shape, and then used the Eraser to fade the far end of the rope out as it reached the horizon.

Presto, a life preserver comes to the rescue over a stormy sea—from the comfort and safety of my studio! This image has become a top seller for Stone.

Dragon

Client: Stock photograph, published by Getty Images

In my younger years, during those long lectures on algebra, I used to doodle—drawing fierce, fire-breathing dragons with elaborate detail. I loved to draw dragons, but somewhere along the way the dragons left me. Fast forward: I am sitting at my desk scribbling down stock ideas. I pause and begin to doodle. A dragon's head appears. Then it hits me. Now I have the capability not just to draw dragons, but to create photo-realistic dragons!

The fire-breathing part wouldn't be difficult. I knew from my pyromaniac childhood that a candle held in front of a can of spray paint would provide the fire (as it had for "Fighting Fire"). The dragon parts? A lizard perhaps—I remembered that my brother owned quite a large iguana. I had a good shot of a castle from a trip to Spain. I also had some cobblestones rescued from street repair in front of my San Francisco studio that would serve as a place for the dragon to stand. A distant shot of the Grand Tetons from a trip to a dude ranch in Wyoming would make a great background.

We started by shooting the iguana in my studio. I had my brother hold it in a variety of positions. In one memorable shot, I actually captured on film a thick gelatinous yellow stream of iguana urine headed directly for the camera. We also constructed and photographed a landing of steps out of the cobblestones. Finally, we photographed the flames from the can of spray paint.

With all of the elements scanned in and ready to go, I sat down at the computer. Where to begin? This is a familiar place for me. Quite often the task at hand seems impossible. How the heck do I create a dragon out of an iguana? I used the Liquify filter on a head shot to stretch out and reshape the iguana's head. Once I had taken that process as far as I could without destroying the integrity of the file, I duplicated the layer and repositioned it to further lengthen the jaws. I created the neck from the tail.

For the spines on the dragon's back and its teeth, I Pen-tooled the
iguana's back, inverted the selection, and deleted the extra material. I
pasted the castle behind the dragon's body and gave the background a
slight blur to give it a dreamy quality.

The image has proven to be one of my most popular among 12-year-
old boys. As for the iguana, he eventually escaped from my brother's
house and is probably looking for an animal-rights lawyer to sue me for
residuals.

Woman at the Helm

Client: Stock photograph, published by Getty Images

"Woman at the Helm" is another image I wanted to do for a long time before I got around to it. My original plan had been to rent a ship's wheel and set up the shot in my studio. I would have a wind machine and lots of spray bottles of water. I'd shoot the model fighting the gale, hands gripping the wheel as the wind and sea-spray tore at her hair. I'd add the stormy sky afterwards. Somehow, though, I never quite got around to it.

Eventually I met a fellow photographer, a woman who lived on a boat with her husband. One day she suggested they take me out sailing. The image resurfaced in my mind. I checked to make sure her boat had the right kind of steering wheel. I hired an assistant, Jayma, to be our model, bought some wet-weather gear for her, rented my friend's boat (and sailing services), and set a date to cast off. The San Francisco Bay in summer is almost invariably fogged in, which would be perfect for the shot because the light would be similar to a storm. Plus, the fog would obscure visual cues such as the city skyline.

Problem was, the day of the shoot was perfect—no fog!

We decided to go for it anyway. If nothing else, we would have an enjoyable day of sailing. Then I figured it out: To get the right quality of light, I directed the captain to sail the boat back and forth under the Golden Gate Bridge. In the bridge shadows we had the same cool, indirect light as under a cloudy sky.

I exposed about 24 sheets of 4 by 5 film to get the look I wanted. When the film came back I had one shot of her face with the right expression and in focus—and one shot with the hands in the right position and properly out-of-focus. I merged the two shots and the background sky with layer masks.

Other than ending up seasick from trying to focus a 4 by 5 camera in the cabin of a tossing boat, the shoot turned out to be a terrific success. The image sold three times in the month I wrote this.

Woman Atlas

Client: Stock photograph, published by Corbis

I read an article in the paper about working mothers. It described the difficulty of balancing work and home and how this feat was fundamentally changing our society. It seemed like a good concept for stock—but how to show it? The phrase *carrying the weight of the world on her shoulders* popped into my head. That was it: a female Atlas.

The model was perfect for my shot. She was a body builder with an incredible, muscular physique, but she was very feminine and pretty at the same time. She had long curly hair, and when she put it up for the shot it looked like the hair one sees on Greek and Roman statues.

One of my fundamental problems was how to deal with the background. If Atlas is carrying the Earth, then where is she standing? The less literal I was about this the better, I decided. Perhaps I could have her legs disappearing into fog. I began to sort through my files. I found a shot taken from an airplane window as I came in for a landing at SFO. A blue expanse showed above the clouds.

To make sure that I got the model's hands in the right position, I had her hold the canopy of an opened umbrella so her arms were on either side, as if holding a large ball. The umbrella was supported by a light stand, which gave her a round object to use for hand placement. In the final composite I replaced the umbrella with a NASA shot of Earth, supplied by my stock agency.

When I showed the image to the agency the only change they requested was to cover the model's buttocks with some "fog." The image was also used for a book cover. In that case the book designer had me *add* breasts to the model.

At one point I was standing behind two men who were viewing the image at an exhibit. One man said, "I know when an image has been digitally done. This one has not been digitally altered!" How, I wondered, would I have done this image without digitally manipulating it?

Stampede!

Client: Stock photograph, published by Getty Images

For years had I wanted to do a stampede of longhorn cattle. I felt it would be an exciting image that could be used to illustrate the popularity of something, or mass hysteria, or even out-of-control situations. But the logistics of such an image seemed enormous. Then one day, while shooting some cats with an animal trainer, I asked her if she could find a herd of longhorn cattle. "Sure," she said, "I know of a herd about an hour from here." I immediately asked her to set it up.

To shoot the stampeding cattle, I purchased several six-pack-sized coolers and cut holes into the sides. In each one I placed a Nikon with wide-angle lenses and autoexposure and a remote firing device. When we got to the ranch, I told the owner that I wanted to set the cameras up in the pasture, then drive the cattle over them while I triggered the cameras remotely. "Won't work," she said. "Why not?" I inquired. She said the cattle would be too wary. They would see the coolers and give them a wide berth. Undaunted I suggested that we could place the coolers next to the posts on each side of a gate, disguise them with weeds, and drive the longhorns through the gates. "Won't work," she said. "They still won't go near 'em." I asked if we could try anyway and she agreed.

After we set up the cameras, the owner began herding the cattle toward the gate. While not exactly stampeding, at least they were trotting at a good pace—that is, until they got within about 15 feet of the gate. At that point they came to a screeching halt. After much urging by the owner, one by one they slipped cautiously through the gate—at least until I used the remote to fire a camera off. At the barely audible noise they turned and ran the other way.

Plan B. We would place a bucket of grain in front of a steer; then I would get up close with a 20mm wide-angle lens. When I was ready, the owner would sneak up behind the animal and slap it in the rear with an empty grain sack. Now these are huge beasts, with horns that measure 6 feet from tip to tip, but the owner was adamant that it was pretty safe—that even when startled, the longhorns would not want to run into or over me.

Despite my doubts, I crouched down about 3 or 4 feet in front of one
of the happily munching steers. As the owner began to swing her empty
grain sack I began to shoot. The startled steer lurched past me and I
fell onto my butt—a process we repeated about 30 times with different
animals. But we got our shots. After that, we put a leaf blower into the
dirt road and shot more film of the resulting dust clouds.

Back in the studio we Pen-tooled about 15 of the cattle and began to
copy and paste them into a single image. Then began the long, arduous
process of working with layer masks to paint the animals in and out,
along with the dust, until we had a convincing stampede image. For the
background we used a bluff that I shot in New Mexico.

Resources

There are many sources of information available about Adobe Photoshop and photography. Here are some recommendations:

Note: As we went to press, Adobe announced Photoshop CS. The information in this book still applies. Most of the books below will be updated for the new version.

Books

Blatner, David and Bruce Fraser, *Real World Adobe Photoshop 7* (Peachpit Press, 2002)
> Two experts delve into the print production side of Photoshop.

Caponigro, John Paul, *Adobe Photoshop Master Class: John Paul Caponigro,* 2d ed. (Adobe Press, 2003)
> Erudite photographer explains his approach to photocomposition.

Eismann, Katrin, *Photoshop Restoration and Retouching,* 2d ed. (New Riders Publishing, to be published 2004)
> Photographer and educator shows step by step how to salvage images.

Kelby, Scott, *The Photoshop Book for Digital Photographers* (New Riders Publishing, 2003)
> The man behind the National Association of Photoshop Professionals places Photoshop in the context of digital cameras.

McClelland, Deke, *The Photoshop 7 Bible* (John Wiley & Sons, 2002)
Big, fat, and comprehensive—written by one of the best educators in the business.

Monroy, Bert, *Photoshop Studio with Bert Monroy* (New Riders Publishing, 2002)
Amazing digital artist reveals his photorealistic painting techniques.

Pfiffner, Pamela, *Inside the Publishing Revolution: The Adobe Story* (Adobe Press, 2002)
Coauthor of the book you're holding explains the origin of Photoshop and the evolution of Adobe (includes interviews with John Lund).

Romaniello, Steve, *Photoshop 7 Savvy* (Sybex, 2002)
Straightforward and to the point, with a clean layout and good indexes.

Steuer, Sharon, *Creative Thinking in Photoshop: A New Approach to Digital Art* (New Riders Publishing, 2002)
Digital illustrator takes an unconventional approach to Photoshop—that is, think like an artist.

Web Sites

Information and resources

Advertising Photographers of America (www.apanational.org)
Offers business resources and software for pro photographers, links to local chapters, and forums on digital topics.

American Society of Media Photographers (www.asmp.org)
Among the resources it offers is the *Copyright Guide for Photographers.*

Creativepro.com (www.creativepro.com)
Complete online resource for creative professionals offers news, how-tos, and reviews of Photoshop and digital cameras.

Digital Photography Review (www.dpreview.com)
Up-to-date and thorough digital camera reviews.

Imaging Revue (www.imagingrevue.com)
A consortium of Photoshop experts gives advice and answers questions for a fee.

National Association of Photoshop Professionals
(www.photoshopuser.com)
Birds of a feather flock together.

Photo District News (www.pdnonline.com)
Online version of the bible for professional photographers; includes a section called "PIX" that focuses on digital techniques.

Photoshop Techniques (www.photoshoptechniques.com)
Cool tips, techniques, and discussion forums for Photoshop geeks.

Rob Galbraith DPI (www.robgalbraith.com)
Pro-level resource with digital camera news, reviews, and forums.

United States Copyright Office (www.copyright.gov/)
The place to copyright your work—and make sure you're not violating others' copyrighted work.

ZoneZero (www.zonezero.com)
Photographer Pedro Meyer's unique vision always leaves you wondering what is a realistic fabrication and what is weird but real.

Stock images

Getty Images (www.gettyimages.com)
Huge offering of royalty-free and rights-protected images, includes sub-brands like Stone, Photodisc, and EyeWire.

CMCD Visual Symbols Library (www.visualsymbols.com)
From designer Clement Mok's company, contemporary images, many of them silhouetted objects.

Corbis (www.corbis.com)

Offers both royalty-free and rights-protected images; features world-famous Bettmann Archive and other collections.

fStop (www.fstopimages.com)

Unusual and artistic collection from designers and artists such as David Byrne, David Carson, and April Greiman.

Veer (www.veer.com)

Images both practical and eclectic from a variety of stock boutiques, including fStop and Solus.

Workbookstock (www.workbookstock.com)

The digital incarnation of the photographer's sourcebook, which now sells stock imagery.

Index

printing
    converting files to CMYK, 32
    quality check with, 30–31
    resolution for, 25

Q

quality
    checking on, 30–31
    digital cameras, 22–23

R

Radial Zoom Blur, 187, 192–195
Reconstruct tool, 176
reflections, 11–12, 208–209
Rescue photo, 282–283
reshaping natural elements, 148–162
    The Devil photo, 149
    image parts, 150–151
    image process, 152–156
    layers, 157
    with Liquify brush, 158–162
resolution, 23–25
resources, information, 292–295
Reveal All command, 28, 111
RGB files, 31–32
Riders photo, 41
rights-managed images, 17
Rooster photo. *see* color, creating new
    realities
royalty-free collections, 17, 18

S

saturation. *see* Hue/Saturation
Save Path command, 58
saving
    with alpha channels, 73
    paths, 58
scale, 38
scanning resolution, 23–24
shadows, 250–268
    adding dimension, 178, 191
    creating rounded reflections, 208–
        209
    fine-tuning, 11–12, 29–30
    image parts, 252–253
    image process, 254–258
    with layer masks, 260–267
    layers, 259
    overview of, 250
    Pool Dog photo, 251
    realism, 261
    Riders photo, 49
shadows, Dominatrix photo
    adding monitor head, 129, 142–143

creating light and, 132–133
    fine-tuning, 137–138
sharpening, 29–30
shutter speed, 13
size
    brush, 27
    with Free Transform tool, 59, 174,
        180, 203, 221, 223, 244
    reducing with flattening, 31
    trimming with Pen tool, 92–93
Skew command, 91
Smudge tool, 263
"spare parts"
    archiving, 17–19
    buying, 17, 294–295
    legal issues, 18–19
    shooting, 14–16
speed, 192–195
Spherize filter, 203, 206–209
SRL (Survival Research Laboratories),
    218
Stampede! photo, 290–291
stock image resources, 294–295

T

Tech Woman photo. *see* dimensional
    distortion
Transform tools
    Distort, 85, 90–94, 99, 129
    Free Transform. *see* Free Transform
    overview of, 38
    positioning layers, 78–79
transparencies
    changing opacity, 230
    using film for large, 23
trimming, 92–93

V

vectors, 51–52
Visual Symbols Library, 19
visualization, 10

W

Warp tool, 175, 179
Web site resources, 293–294
Woman at the Helm photo, 286–287
Woman Atlas photo, 288–289

Z

Zoom setting, Radial Blur, 192–195, 203